GLOWING

AFTER THE

DARKNESS

GLOWING AFTER THE DARKNESS

HANNAH LEASURE

TATE PUBLISHING
AND ENTERPRISES, LLC

Published by Tate Publishing & Enterprises, LLC
127 E. Trade Center Terrace | Mustang, Oklahoma 73064 USA
1.888.361.9473 | www.tatepublishing.com

Tate Publishing is committed to excellence in the publishing industry. The company reflects the philosophy established by the founders, based on Psalm 68:11,

"The Lord gave the word and great was the company of those who published it."

Book design copyright © 2016 by Tate Publishing, LLC. All rights reserved.
Cover design by Joshua Rafols
Interior design by Shieldon Alcasid

Published in the United States of America

ISBN: 978-1-68293-959-8
Biography & Autobiography / Personal Memoirs
16.01.28

To my friend Noah, the kids at St. Jude,
and all who have battled cancer
your courage has inspired me to live
every day with meaning

Acknowledgments

I DEDICATE THIS book to the Lord, for he is good. He has shown me that no matter what obstacles you go through, he will be right there—not only to protect you but to heal you as well. He is my safe place throughout this journey and gives me hope. He opened my eyes; life isn't just given to you, you're here for a specific purpose. He gave me a second chance at life and an opportunity to share my testimony. I didn't get better because of time, I got better because he was right there with me telling me that everything was going to be okay, and he helped me to persevere through the deepest, darkest times. He was my light in a dark place. I give him all the praise.

I want to thank my parents and family for keeping the faith and for believing in my healing.

Thank you to my hometown of Toronto and all the amazing people who prayed and held fundraisers for me.

Thank you to Dr. Blackburn and Dr. Alper, who have had a significant hand in my medical care.

Finally to Christian Life Missions and the youth group in Puerto Rico, thank you for fervently praying for hours for my healing. God heard your prayer. Thank you for showing me the power of prayer is real.

Contents

Senior Year

IT'S FINALLY HERE: my senior year of high school. These will be the final days of walking through these tall glass double doors that adorn the entry way to my soon-to-be alma mater. These are the final months of scurrying to my locker then to my homeroom before the tardy bell rings. This will be my last year of putting on that red and silver uniform and cheering in front of hundreds of dedicated fans on those crisp fall days. I have been cheering since I turned seven years old. I have always had that bubbly personality that enjoys socializing with others.

All of a sudden, it hit me: this will be my last of everything, particularly my last year in choir. Oh, how I love to sing, and I have an alto voice that can hit the really high notes. In the final year, I will participate in musicals. I have enjoyed the many roles I have been honored to play. Last year I was Auntie Em and the good witch. I had an amazing time with the other members of the cast. We are a musical family that goes beyond the auditions, rehearsals, and the actual performances. We enjoy watching movies and having pizza night and attending musicals as a group. I will definitely miss this time in my life and hope to be a good role model for the younger kids who will soon take my place.

Sports memorabilia adorn all areas of the school from football to baseball to golf; you name it, there's a decoration for it. This town is known for its sports program and has had some talented people come out of here. The words to our alma mater and the Pledge of Allegiance hang from the high newly renovated ceilings. I can't even fathom how many times I recited the Alma Mater. This will forever be etched in my brain. I remember the memory like it was yesterday, walking into my first day of preschool and clinging frantically to my mom, only to be handed over to one of the greatest teachers I will ever know, Ms. Popejoy who loved every child as though they were her own. She had a warm and welcoming smile that just made this petite blue-eyed girl with golden locks feel secure. As I stand in the foyer of my high school reminiscing about such sweet childhood memories and reviewing all my accomplishments as well as the quality time invested in me by so many wonderful teachers, I vow to be the most inspiring role model to the other students who will follow.

It hasn't always been glamorous. Of course, when you have so many female peers in one class, it can get a little annoying and catty at times. Everyone seems to try to surpass the others in appearance, boyfriends, and extracurricular activities. We are definitely a superficial breed and do not appear to be bearing the right kind of fruit. I have been brought up in church but have lost my focus on the spiritual things of God. I have always considered myself a caring and compassionate person, but I know that this is not enough to make it to heaven.

I have had several close friendships and have helped these girls with interpersonal conflicts with each other and with their boyfriends. I always thought that I should be a therapist; I enjoy listening to and helping others work through their problems. These same girls at times would decide to ignore me, which I believe is one of the cruelest forms of bullying: silent bullying. I have been made to feel isolated and rejected at times. Situations would arise at the lunch table that would cause me to eat my lunch in the bathroom stall or in a classroom.

I do hope this year will be better and that we all have matured since last year. This is the year that we should model to the underclassmen how to interact with others and what it means to be an exemplary student. I am once again elected class secretary of the student senate. I enjoy working with the others to coordinate events for the senior class and to decorate these long pale gray hallways and scarlet lockers that seem to be rusting a little more as each new year begins.

Pictures adorn the walls of students past, so many stories each one can tell of their high school experience. There she is—my great-grandmother, of the class of 1934. How her brown eyes sparkle with vitality, her pale, milky white complexion looking flawless. My class, the class of 2014, will soon be joining them. Amazing how time goes by so quickly, and I am determined to make this the most memorable year of my life.

Looking over my class schedule, I see this will be a very busy and exciting year. Algebra is not one of my best subjects, but when it comes to campaigning for money, I am a real philanthropist. In the past, I have enjoyed raising money to help senior class events, relay for life, and other organizations. This year, we will be rallying for trauma bears for the kids at the children's hospital. I have a tender heart for sick kids, and I hope that I will be able to deliver these in person. I must admit that my brain is brilliant when it comes to helping others in this capacity.

First period is choir. Oh, how I love to sing, God has blessed me with a beautiful alto voice that, I must add, was inherited to me from my dad, who is the worship leader in our church. Every year, we present a Christmas concert and present one again in the spring. I am so excited to try out for a solo and will cherish these final concerts.

My schedule consists of art class, another strong class for me. I enjoy painting wildlife and using acrylic paints to bring out a boldness and texture to my subject. It is definitely a rewarding experience to see your painting on display for the surrounding communities to view at the annual art exhibit.

Business management will be beneficial since my goal is to open my own beauty salon one day. I already have the name for my salon and will promote "locks of love" due to the fact that several of my family members have been afflicted with some form of cancer. I remember that it was April 2011. I had just finished school for the day and had received a phone call from my grandma who informed me that she had breast cancer. I immediately drove to her house, sat with her, and hugged her, not ever wanting to let her go. I remember praying and asking God to heal her and saying that I needed more time with her. It was difficult seeing her lose her hair from the chemotherapy and radiation. I never want to go through anything like that.

Autumn Homecoming

AUTUMN BRINGS ANOTHER homecoming to this quaint, small town. While strolling down these old-fashioned brick roads, you will find posters and streamers hanging from lampposts scattered throughout the town. The residents dress in their sports apparel and come together to support our hometown athletes. Some have referred to us as the "Little Mayberry" on the Ohio River. In the center of town, we have a large gazebo painted in flat old lace white with *azul* trimmings. An American flag flies from the central hub, and smaller flags drape over the beams. A colorful flock of monkey-faced pansies and bright yellow trumpet daffodils surround the perimeter. We have many gatherings here for community fund-raisers to memorial services. This has been quite the landmark for photo shoots for our school dances.

This will be the final year of dress shopping with Mom. It is always the exciting adventure to explore new shops to find that perfect, one-of-a-kind dress. A manicure and pedicure is a must, and of course, so is the perfect hairstyle. The girls in town go all out and make every dance a memorable one. I have attended every dance since my freshman year, not allowing anything to keep me from them. Homecoming is here, and I pray I make this year's homecoming court, as it has always been Mom's dream for me to be homecoming queen. I believe it to be true when they say that parents tend to live their dreams through the lives of their children.

Five girls will be selected from the senior class that consists of thirty. This would be such an honor and the icing on the cake to top off my senior year. There are so many popular and attractive girls, but I feel confident due to my involvement in activities and a good attitude towards others. I have already pictured in my head the dress I would love to wear on that day, an ombre pink gown that starts light at the top, and as it cascades down, the pink shades become more intense. The bodice will be embellished with silver gems and a corset backing.

My schedule continues to pile up, but I wouldn't want it any other way. Track, softball, stat girl for wrestling, and being the yearbook editor is a few more activities that I enjoy doing. Taking pictures of the class and capturing those awkward moments that make us an original and peculiar group is very rewarding.

I was elected "Best Hair" in junior high. My hair has always been thick in texture and is such a pretty blonde color. Styling is a strength of mine, and I have always been unpredictable in my appearance. The color of my hair changes as the seasons change, but what girl doesn't want to experiment with different colors?

I enjoy going to the urban mission and attending youth group at my church, but I think I will have to postpone some of the church activities. God knows my heart, and he will understand that this is a busy year and that I have good intentions in wanting to help others.

Gazing at the bulletin board, I notice that musical tryouts will be Monday after school. I wonder if I'll get the lead role this year. This will be my fifth and final performance. Participating in musicals has combined my love for music and my love for acting into one incredible experience. This year's performance will be my favorite Disney classic: Beauty and the Beast. I was born to play Belle. My golden locks can easily be changed to chestnut brown curls cascading down to a beautiful buttercup yellow gown.

Monday will be here before I know it, so it looks like I will be busy practicing for my rehearsal. Music has always been my passion, and when my grandmother was battling cancer, I was able to use my strong alto voice and sing a special song to her and the congregation. I made it through the entire song before I broke down, but I knew I had to be strong for her and the family.

Sunday morning and it's time to get ready for church, but I just want to pull my warm, fuzzy, leopard print blanket over my head and go back to sleep. This past weekend has been exhausting, going from party to party with my friends. Unfortunately, I am starting to pick up some bad habits to try to feel accepted. This behavior is totally against what we have believed in, but I find myself sinking more and more into this dangerous pit.

My parents have raised me in church and have tried to instill Christian values into my siblings and I. We attended Sunday school and youth group. My dad has been the worship leader since before I was born and has been on the board of directors as well as an adult Sunday school teacher. I hope he is not disappointed in my relationship with God. I know that God understands how busy I am and that I do a lot to help others.

Overall, I am a very good person and have a high respect for others and enjoy heading up fund-raisers for those who are sick, especially kids with cancer. One day, I hope to visit St. Jude's Hospital and visit some of the children to show them my support and to give them hope. For as long as I can remember, my parents have donated faithfully to this hospital for cancer research, stating this is the charity that God has put on their heart.

I don't know if I will ever get to make a trip to Memphis and visit this hospital, but I know this is near and dear to my heart; and if there is a time when my parents can no longer donate, I will continue this very important cause. Cancer tends to run in my family, and I hope that I can somehow make a difference and carry on this tradition in generations to come.

Monday brings another busy week at school. Today musical tryouts will be taking place after school. I am a little apprehensive with this being my final year performing and will be competing against so many other talented girls for the lead role. What better production to end my musical career than that of Belle in" Beauty and the Beast? This movie is one of my favorite Disney classics, and I have watched it time and time again with my mom, who is also a big fan. There is something about a love and romance that keeps me mesmerized. It is every girl's dream to feel like a princess and to live in a big castle with a handsome prince.

My dad has also performed various roles in high school musicals and has had lead roles. I get my singing and acting capabilities from him. My family is talented in singing and playing musical instruments. One day, I hope to play the piano and sing at church.

Auditions are beginning; I chose the song I dedicated to my maw maw when she was battling breast cancer two years ago. I hope this song will make a big impact on the four judges who will be scrutinizing our every note. This is difficult, knowing this is my last tryout and last performance with this cast. I have grown to love each of them, and we consider each other family and will always be here to support one another.

We have worked together to raise money for each performance's special scenery and costumes for each cast member. We have always looked forward to getting together and having pizza while painting the scenes and coming up with brilliant ideas for props. We have dedicated months to practices and preparation. Looking back on all the previous shows, I can honestly say that each one has been a success and that this community looks forward to attending and are very supportive.

Here we go. I'm up, and I feel nauseous; but I have to stay calm so my voice will project and resonate without breaking. It is not an easy task to sing a cappella, but it is required by the judges. I have been noted to be called a triple threat, which is a compliment on the musical level. It refers to those who can sing, dance, and act, which is needed in this competition.

My audition for Belle went well. I was able to hit the high notes and seemed to impress the judges by the expression on their faces. I feel pretty confident with my performance, and knowing this chapter of my life is one for the history books makes me feel heavyhearted.

The results are posted. I reluctantly walk to the board with my mind preoccupied with thoughts of rejection. What if I didn't get the lead? I will be so disappointed and discouraged, but I could never stop singing as this brings me so much comfort and elation. If I made it, I will be dedicating several hours each night for rehearsal and helping the younger ones with their part in this drama.

I finally and hesitantly arrive at the bulletin board. My eyes scroll down the list of characters, and once I located Belle, I placed my finger, which is shaking awkwardly, on the name and move it slowly to the right until I reach the name of the individual who made lead. It was me! I made the lead role! Although it is ephemeral, I am so excited and can't help but shriek loudly and feeling like I could jump ten feet in the air. Well, there's no time to waste. The production is four months away in February, and I want to get started immediately. These next four months will be unforgettable.

Autumn is my favorite time of year. I love wearing my oversized sweatshirts while roasting marshmallow and carving pumpkins with my family. We look forward to going to a local pumpkin patch and picking out our own personal pumpkins to carve. Our home has been host to many bonfires for my friends and also for singing around the campfire while my dad plays the guitar.

The fall foliage always seems to be so vibrant in the country with the sun enhancing all the brilliant colors of each individual leaf. Looking at this splendor shows the magnificence of God's artistry and masterpiece. Each season brings its own beauty and personal memories.

October brings the selection of this year's homecoming court. This is such an exciting time; the senior class will select five girls out of thirty to represent Toronto High. There will be a pep rally today as part of the homecoming festivities. I hope I get to be one of the five girls selected. My mom would be so thrilled; she has told me since I was a little girl that she would love for me to be homecoming queen.

The pep rally will take place today at one o'clock in the gymnasium. This will surely be the longest morning ever. I don't know how I will be able to concentrate on my studies as my mind is preoccupied with today's events.

It is lunchtime, and I cannot eat a thing or I'll be sick. There's no room for food amongst all these butterflies in my stomach. All I can do is glance at the clock and pray that time would move quicker. Soon I will be elated or completely disheartened and disappointed. How would I break the news to my mom? It has to be every little girl's dream to be queen of her alma mater.

This is a glamorous and magical time that is not experienced by many. The other girls seem so calm. Or are they disguising it well? The gym doors are opening, and the students are filing in.

As I take my seat on the cool wooden bleachers, I think about all the queens who have come and went. Will this be my year to represent our class? Looking around the gym, I realize this will soon be a distant memory as I will be heading to college in less than a year. I will be in a new atmosphere that I am unaccustomed to, but I am ready to start a new journey that will help others to feel good about themselves and their appearance, especially those inflicted with cancer. I could not imagine losing my hair. It would be devastating and take a drastic blow on self-esteem.

I believe that if you feel good about your appearance, your self-confidence will be exemplified and would, in return, cause joy and happiness. To see my clients smile will reflect the internal feelings and attitude outwardly for all to see.

The principal is ready to announce the candidates. I can't help but move my legs back and forth in a nervous fashion. The principal has always been a fair and approachable leader who makes students feel comfortable. On many occasions, I would find myself sitting in her office in an uncomfortable chair, bringing forth my issues I was having with some of the other girls. Unfortunately, that chair became all too familiar to me.

There were days I dreaded coming to school knowing I would find myself in "girl theatrics" that I couldn't seem to avoid. If it wasn't fighting over someone else's boyfriend, it was trying to make ourselves look better by criticizing someone else or discounting their abilities as a cheerleader. We seemed to put too much emphasis on outward appearance and popularity, which seems to be a survival mechanism amongst high school girls.

"May I have your attention please! We are ready to announce the homecoming court for 2013. Please everyone take your seats. This is an exciting moment for these girls who will be representing our high school this month as queen candidates. These girls are very involved in activities such as fund-raising and sports and have shown a willingness to help others and to be role models for our underclassmen. The five girls are…"

I couldn't believe it! My name was the first one to be announced. I took my place on the gym room floor in front of all the other students. What an honor to represent my school in this capacity. I felt like I was in a dream, and it felt so amazing. I see my brother, who is a freshman, cheering me on from the stands. We have a good relationship and have always been there for each other. I will never forget this moment, and I hope to be a good role model for the remainder of this school year.

My parents were so excited. To carry on the tradition of this town, we decorated the house with congratulatory decorations. Pink and black were the colors I chose, and I will soon be looking for my gown to wear on the field.

I am two months into my senior year, and it has already been filled with so many wonderful and exciting events. I am so blessed to have all these opportunities that not many get to experience. I will be getting senior pictures done this weekend and will have the beautiful autumn foliage as my background.

Winter pictures will be in a few months, and I already have my wardrobe picked out for this.

What a great year this is already, and it only has begun. I am having the time of my life, and I look forward to participating in all the upcoming school dances. I love to dress up, and I enjoy dancing. I have not missed one in four years. The winter ball also known as "band formal" is one of my favorite dances, and it will take place in February 2014. But first, we have to get through homecoming.

Another weekend celebrating with my friends doesn't mix well with Sunday morning church. Our pastor is a wonderful man of God, but I seem to not be able to concentrate on the sermon. My mind is wondering on the things I need to do after church today. My mother and I are driving to a charming little dress shop in search of the perfect homecoming dress.

I have an image of how I want my dress to look: pink ombre gown beginning with magenta and cascading down into a lighter shade of blush pink. The bodice will be embellished with silver metallic gems and a corset backing, and long white gloves and silver accessories will complete the ensemble. I am thankful for my thick sandy blonde hair and have always been complimented on my appearance.

I'm not one to be so superficial. I believe it's important to exercise and to eat wholesome foods to have a healthy self-esteem. I heard my pastor say our bodies are the temple of the Holy Spirit. I have learned something in church after all.

Reflection

Looking back on my childhood, it was surrounded by friends and family who have always inspired and encouraged me to pursue my dreams and to always give God the glory for each day, good or bad. Would I be able to give God glory in the midst of a storm or would I buckle or prevail? I have not found myself in such a place to determine the outcome and hope I never do. I recollect a saying that goes "You don't wait for the storm to pass." There's another that says "You learn to dance in the rain."

Speaking of dancing as a child, I was such a diva—some things never change—dancing and singing as though I was performing in front of a thousand fans. I was outgoing and always seemed to have a glow and smile that would light up a room. I had the perfect white teeth that seemed to compliment my beaming smile.

My grandfather told me the thing he remembers most about me was the unbelievable steadiness and balance in my motor skills. As a toddler who is just beginning to walk, I wasn't clumsy and was able to reset my balance, preventing me from tumbling. I skipped crawling and immediately advanced to cruising at the age of nine months, the earliest one out of my two siblings.

My mother decided to place me in gymnastics at the age of five, where I quickly learned how to do the perfect cartwheel and the jumps necessary for a career in cheerleading, which began at the age of seven and continuing until the end of this season. Performing in a state competition took a lot of work, but it was something I will never forget.

I am now seventeen years old and feel like I have gained some wisdom over the years. Time is fleeting and what we have done in our life time will make a positive and lasting impression or will only chalk up to a mere existence.

While growing up, I have always loved to jump and have had unbelievable strength in my calves from all the exercise associated with gymnastics and cheering. My parents bought me a large screened-in trampoline, and I would spend hours out on our two acres lot jumping and doing flips. I would sit when I became tired and daydream about how much I had to look forward to in my life.

I remember one time I was lying on the trampoline and wondering how my senior year of high school would be. I had wondered then if everything I wanted to be and do would come to pass. I often thought about college and what I wanted to do after high school. I love to feel beautiful and would enjoy making others feel this way as well. Would I be a cosmetologist and help those inflicted with cancer to feel better about their appearance? I had many aspirations on that trampoline.

I also thought about how amazing it would be to have a little sister to dress up and to use as a guinea pig for new hairdos and makeup lessons. So when my parents had a boy, I wasn't thrilled at first, but I decided to practice manicures on him. He didn't seem to mind when I colored his nails pink.

My brother and I have grown to have such a close relationship, I remember always wanting to feed him and take care of him when he was a baby. We have grown up helping each other through struggles and rejoicing in each other's victories. I have given him girl advice and vice versa. It is necessary to have a good support system and someone who will pick you up when you are down. I wouldn't change him for ten sisters.

Sunday school has always been a big part of our lives as kids. We would not only attend on Sundays but on midweek as well, participating in Royal Rangers and God's girls. My favorite song that I grew up singing was "Amazing Grace." The story behind it is inspiring, and I have always seemed to find comfort in it. I have participated in music at church where we would perform sign language dances, which was a different twist on singing but a blessing as well.

Easter and Christmas brought church plays, and summer time brought Bible school. My parents have always tried to instill Christ in us, knowing that this is vital for a prosperous and pleasing life. As a family, we made it a point to enjoy Sundays at church with a luncheon at a different establishment after the service.

As I grew older, I noticed my relationship with God was lacking, and I was more interested in the things this world had to offer and getting caught up in the circle of popularity. Weekends were made to hang out with friends and experimenting with certain substances that can definitely get you hooked and take your focus off the things of God.

As a way to justify my behavior, I remind myself that I am a good person and that God knows that I have a heart for people, especially those who are developmentally delayed and have autism. One example that comes to mind is when a new student started school and needed someone to orient him to the classrooms. I jumped at the chance and was drawn to him, taking his hand and walking him through the building.

His eyes lit up when he saw we had an elevator. I believe we rode this for fifteen minutes, becoming familiar with each floor over and over again. He immediately trusted me, and we became close friends. Another activity that I will be adding to my list is participating in the Special Olympics as a hugger. I know that God is proud of the person I am. After all, no one is perfect.

Currently, I hit and miss Sunday mornings. I find myself partying on the weekends (which I have made a priority) and sleeping in on Sundays (which I have found is a necessity). When did I start to fall away from my relationship with God? Is it because of this age group, which believes that being a Christian is not cool or accepted by my peers? Is my relationship with him enough to sustain me?

When I look at all the good I have done for others, how can God not be pleased with me and the works that I have accomplished and the relationships I have made? There are so many others who have done a lot worse things in life.

My dad has always prayed and continues to do so today for a revival in Toronto. His prayer is that there is a newsworthy story in this town that will bring about a miraculous event from which only God can receive the glory. I think my dad is in a fantasy world, but he perseveres in this prayer, even sharing this with others. He states that when this comes to pass, there will be many new believers.

What could spark a revival in this town of about five thousand that would make such a change in the community? How could God receive such glory? And would it spread to neighboring towns? I'll believe it when I see it.

It was October 10. What a beautiful fall day for a homecoming! The vibrant leaves swirled in a gentle wind, and there was an unusually warm temperature for this time of year. This is the day I have been waiting for since the first time I walked into preschool. This has always been a dream of mine, and it has finally arrived. God could not have blessed us with a more perfect day to enjoy the festivities.

Today will be filled with activities from sunrise to sunset. Our classes will be shortened to prepare for this annual event that attracts hundreds of spectators. Students are sporting their shirts today in support of their favorite candidate. It is humbling to see so many "Team Hannah" shirts floating around the school, suggesting that somehow I made an impact on that individual displaying it. This will be the only time I see others wearing shirts to support my cause, and I am very thankful.

Our pep rally successfully launched an anticipation of these evening events. I had my picture taken in my cheering uniform that will be displayed on a banner for senior night. This will be another amazing event at the end of the football season where I will be escorted by both my parents across the football field for the last time. I have enjoyed every activity that I have participated in and will be grateful for every moment ahead. Soon these will be only memories.

It was time to check off my list; my hair was done, my nails and makeup were done, and I had purchased candy for the parade and picked up my pink rose bouquet from the florist. Now it was time to get into my pink ombre gown with a hoop under it. Of course, this type of dress can never be too full. My parents are dressed in pink and black, and my other family members in their "Team Hannah" shirts. I am ready to take my place in the parade caravan.

Upon arriving at the stadium, I view numerous people wearing shirts with my name on it, hoping that tonight I receive the tiara. Just to be selected by my classmates as a candidate is an honor, but being crowned queen would be amazing and something that I wouldn't take lightly. This to me would mean that I should improve even more on how to be a good leader, especially for those who want to follow in my footsteps.

Each candidate takes their place on their designated convertible decorated with signs—some professionally crafted and others homemade—on each door. My white basket with pink faux lining is overflowing with an assortment of candy, ready to be tossed to all those anticipating our arrival through town.

Little girls line up for their turn to have pictures taken with the queen candidates. A little blonde-haired blue-eyed girl, who reminded me of myself, approached me and asked for my autograph. I feel like a movie star. I hope that I am someone that they can always look up to and can mentor.

The parade is starting as I sit here on my faux white blanket and freshly waxed candy apple red convertible. I can't help but drink in every moment as this has been a long-awaited aspiration.

I wave to all the spectators who have been eagerly awaiting our arrival and gaze upon the faces of children scurrying into the streets to gather up the variety of candy and memorable trinkets, which is the highlight of the parade for them. Hearing the crowds of people shout my name in support of a victory is quite a humbling experience.

Our parade consists of many participants from the community led by the grand marshall and our mayor and followed by the marching band, dancers, flag girls, cheerleaders, football players, and our first responders. This town always comes together in support for one another.

My nerves are getting the best of me, and even though this is such a spectacular time, I am looking forward to having the halftime show over with. I look forward to a weekend of celebration with my friends and attending a few parties.

Upon returning to the stadium, all the candidates have pictures taken together for the yearbook. We represent a rainbow of colors: pink, seafoam green, lilac, navy blue, and royal blue. Each one of us is bringing our own cheer section and hoping that we have the most fans sporting our team shirts. I feel honored to be representing an amazing family and to have my grandparents here to celebrate this special occasion.

One at a time, we line up in front of a stadium full of fans who are ready for the game and the crowning of the 2013 homecoming queen, who tonight will start her reign. What a legacy to leave for future classes. If I have a daughter one day, she will see a yearbook full of pictures with me wearing the tiara.

All the fathers of the candidates await their daughters' arrival and will escort them to the middle of the football field, where the selection of the roses will take place. My dad takes me by the hand; and as they call my name, he walks me to the middle of the field, which my dad is very familiar with due to years of playing the French horn in the high school marching band. Little did he know then that he would one day walk across the field with his little girl.

As we slowly take our place and await the arrival of the other candidates and their fathers, I look into the stands full of alumni and their families and imagine what it would be like to one day be here with my family for another homecoming celebration. I will never forget how I felt at that moment.

We are now being joined on the fields by our mothers. My mother's countenance is that of nervous excitement. She has waited and talked about this moment since I was a little girl. She always had me dressed in the popular styles because as a child she didn't have the nicest clothes and wanted me to have what she never could. She has always sacrificed for her children to give us a good life.

There are five foil-covered roses that will be selected by each father, who will then give it to his daughter. When directed by the master of ceremonies, each candidate will remove the foil. and the one who has the odd-colored rose will be crowned Toronto High School's 2013 homecoming queen.

My dad will be the first one to select, and without hesitation, he knows exactly what rose he wants. He comes back and hands it to me, not knowing if I can even hold on to it due to the fact that my hands are shaking violently. I cannot think of a time I have ever been this nervous.

Each girl has received their flower, and the MC announces, "Girls, you may now open your roses. My mom looks around at the other girls and notices that two of them have yellow roses in their hand. Fumbling with mine, I am unable to get a grip to open it. I hear my mom whisper to me, "You don't want yellow. You don't want yellow."

A third girl has opened a yellow rose. Everyone in the stadium is standing to their feet to get a good look. I feel every eye is on me. I finally grasp the tip of the foil and rip it open to reveal a rose that is colored red. I couldn't believe it. I was in utter shock that I won! I only believed it after the MC announced my name as the new homecoming queen for 2013. The cheers in the stadium were the loudest I have ever heard. I looked around and can't help but feel bad for the other girls.

The silver tiara was dazzling. It had gems covering the front and appeared to be iridescent and shining underneath the Friday night lights. It felt wonderful when they placed it on my head. I will forever cherish this, and one day, I hope to pass it down to my daughter.

When I woke up the next morning, I had to pinch myself. I still felt like it was a dream, but I was actually blessed enough to have it as a reality. Do you think God did this for my mom? Did he give her this gift she had prayed for? This weekend was definitely a time to celebrate with friends, and unfortunately, it also meant sleeping in on Sunday morning.

I have decided I will help our church in feeding the less fortunate a Thanksgiving dinner. I feel good when I help others, but am I doing it out of guilt for not attending church and having a close relationship with God? Maybe I feel like my works will be enough to see me through. Serving others is humbling, and I should be less focused on material things and my appearance and should be more grateful for what I have.

It's difficult to not want to look perfect. I spend so much time preoccupied with my appearance. I make sure my hair is done and that I have the best makeup and clothes. I spend hours reviewing healthy recipes and working out. I want to have an abdomen that is tan and toned for bikini season. It is a necessary evil to keep up with the other girls in appearance. I don't want to be shallow, but I also don't want to be excluded from the popular group.

Unfortunately, it seems like more emphasis is placed on how you perform in sports and how beautiful you are than academic accomplishments. I try to strive to obtain good grades and carry a good average and have even tutored younger students. I am an accomplished reader and excel in science.

Atmosphere of Thanksgiving

NOVEMBER IS HERE, and the air carries the fragrance of blowing and drifting leaves still holding on to their colors. Our home has always been the place where our friends and family gather to celebrate. My mom and I always prepare the menu a couple of weeks in advance, and the guest list seems to grow every year. The one thing I have noticed is that my parents always invite someone from the church who has no place to go for dinner.

I am in charge of the desserts as I seem to have a natural talent for baking and have no fear of trying new recipes. I look forward to this magical time of year and always try to make sure that each celebration is better than the year before. The house is decorated in autumn colors with the scent of a harvest candle permeating throughout. Everyone who comes into our home feels welcomed, and our goal is to be the perfect hosts.

We are on a mission to find the biggest turkey we can, knowing we will have twenty to twenty-five people joining us for dinner. Our menu will consist of mashed potatoes with homemade gravy, dressing that has been handed down to me from my great-grandma, and my nana's delicious cranberry salad. Desserts are overflowing, and the delicious smell of pumpkin pies fills this country kitchen.

My signature dessert is a pumpkin trifle that is layered with spice cake, pumpkin, and homemade whipped topping topped off with roasted pecans. Baking is my favorite pastime, and I will always remember this quality time with my mom.

After Thanksgiving dinner, my mom turns on Christmas music to get everyone in the spirit; and my dad reluctantly digs out our old Christmas tree, even though he would like to take a nap after that Thanksgiving feast. We prepare hot chocolate and begin our excessive decorating. We have many ornaments that have sentimental value, such as the ones we made in preschool that have our pictures on it.

We cover the tree in a variety of ornaments—some old and some new but each one having a story. We spend hours making sure every ornament is perfectly spaced with candy canes in between. I have the honor of placing the angel on the top of the tree. We place neatly wrapped gifts under the tree to complete our decorating.

After the tree is completed, we put in Christmas movies and sit in front of the fireplace. We have a large picture window that displays a beautiful scene when it begins to snow, and the pine trees become covered in a blanket of white.

This is my favorite time of year, as I am able to spend time with my family and continue traditions that I hope to implement when I have my own family. I want to make this the best Christmas ever, thinking of it as possibly the last one with our loved ones. You never know what a year may bring.

On December 2, I walk past my mom's room and see her sitting in front of the computer with tears in her eyes. A song has really touched her heart. When this happens, she listens to it over and over again. She has been listening to this song for a couple of weeks now; the name of the song is "I Heard the Bells on Christmas Day."

My mom explained the story behind this song, which makes it even more incredible. This song was a poem written by Henry Wadsworth Longfellow during the darkest time of the civil war when there seemed to be no reconciliation between the armies. During this time, his wife's dress caught fire from the wax that she used to commemorate a lock of her daughter's hair. He attempted to smother the flames, resulting in him receiving severe burns on his face and that explains the beard after this incident. Sadly, Henry's wife passed away from the burns she sustained. During this time, Henry received a letter stating that his son was severely injured in the war.

He became very depressed and remembered times when bells represented peace, and throughout this trial, Henry Wadsworth Longfellow found peace in the midst of his storm through Christ. Is Jesus somehow preparing my mom for a trial? Why is she so captivated by this song and this poem? Maybe there is no significant purpose for her obsession.

On December 6, I am invited to participate in the county Christmas parade with other homecoming queens from the area high schools. I am honored to meet not only them but also our local and state officials and our local news anchors. I am pleased to be able to represent my hometown of Toronto, and I am thankful that this parade will be televised for my friends and family who could not be here today.

This may be the final parade that I will participate in, but I do not feel sad due to the fact that I'm only three months into my senior year and this has been the most amazing experience that I could have ever imagined. If I do not do another thing, it has been full of self-satisfaction.

As I again sit on my convertible and wave to the crowd, the media is mentioning all my activities and stating how busy I am. They also inform the spectators of all the fund-raisers that I participate in. I love to help those who are ill and the less fortunate to bring some joy to their despondent lives.

This is the first time I have made it on television, and even though it may be the last, I am having the time of my life. This is being captured on video at home, and I will be able to look back on this time one day with my family.

I never could have imagined when I started preschool that when my senior year came, it would be this fabulous and that everything I have learned—my strengths, weaknesses, goals, dreams, and relationships with my teachers and peers—would set a foundation that is built upon every year by my accomplishments in academics and leadership.

Everything we have completed over the years blooms in our senior year, and we leave our legacy for the next class to carry on where we have left off. Each of us look forward to this year and hope that it is all we have ever imagined it would be. The senior year of high school is the greatest year of anyone's school career and the most memorable.

Circuit Overload

IT IS DECEMBER 15. *What a beautiful Sunday afternoon for a Christmas choir concert! Each year, the high school hosts this choir concert to kick off the Christmas season celebration. This year, I will be performing a solo to begin the concert. Each student will hold a candle that will be lit by the person next to them until they are all lit.*

As I stand in front of the crowd singing, I realize that I must be a success when I look on their face and see tears streaming down their face. This is a magical time of year that always brings the community together and makes each heart a little more tender toward one another.

This is my last Christmas choir concert, but I will be participating in the spring concert in March. I always look forward to the spring concert as this signifies the completion of another school year and puts everyone in a good mood for warm weather and baseball season. I have a wonderful choir teacher who has always complimented me on my voice and who has encouraged me to pursue a career in music.

Music is wonderful therapy for me. If I am having a bad day, I put my headphones on, close my eyes, and pretend I'm somewhere else. I have heard that music has brought people out of comas and catatonia-like states. It's amazing to think that music can make such an impact on someone as to bring them out of an unconscious state. I think it would be very rewarding to play music for people who are not responding to other stimuli.

It is December 16, 2013. What is going on with me today that I feel so depressed and even crying at times? I am feeling so overwhelmed with life. My mind is racing, and I am thinking of the things I need to get done before Christmas and all the activities I have scheduled. I have never felt like this and always enjoy every event that I participate in, with my concept being "the more, the merrier."

This is my favorite time of the year, and I should be elated with Christmas and my senior year. My itinerary has always been full,, and I have never had this overwhelming feeling where I actually feel like I need a break. I am at the finish line of my high school career, but I feel like I need a break. I do not understand what is going on. Maybe I am just having a bad day and nothing more.

I drive to my Mawmaw's house and immediately go to her bathroom and sit myself on the floor. I begin sobbing and tell her, "I am in trouble," and I repeat this to her.

"Are you pregnant?" she asks.

"Of course not," I reply. "That's not what I mean. My mind seems foggy, and I feel confused."

I feel irritable and angry, and I find myself cursing and saying things to others that I never would have said in the past. Why am I so mad? And why is my fuse so short? I have been waiting for this time of year to arrive and I have so much I want to do, but my mind is taking over.

I remember constantly holding my head like it was on overload. I approached my mom tearfully and told her I needed a break.

"I can't do all this anymore! I need a break."

My mom, who was very opened to my complaint, recommended that I quit some of my activities. She stated that I should quit all my activities but that she wanted me to continue with a musical.

"How can I quit cheering? This is my last year, and it is one of my favorite activities."

I know my mom is right though; my activities need to stop. I agreed to do a musical; after all, I was finally the lead role, and I wanted more than anything to play the role of Belle. I look forward to musicals every year.

I quit all my activities, hoping this will cure my feeling of confusion and depression. Or did I make it worse by not completing my final year of cheering? After all, I have done this since I was seven. I feel terrible not to finish this through to the end, but I know I cannot.

I have such a terrible headache, and I can't seem to tolerate any lights being on. I need to put a cold compress on my eyes and lie down. I had a terrible headache about a month ago that made me unable to move, and I talked with a clenched jaw.

Maybe all this is just cluster headaches and migraines. If I take some medicine, maybe it will go away. I know we have a family history of migraines. I know this is it. I should be better in no time and can get back to normal and enjoy the holiday.

It is December 18. I feel like I'm getting the stomach flu. I am extremely nauseous and have vomited several times, and I have a low-grade temperature. I call my mom at work, and she brings home soup and clear fluids, also thinking that maybe I am getting a virus. But then she asks me if I could be pregnant. I deny being pregnant, but she still has not ruled that out yet.

I attempt to drink fluids, but I am not able to keep anything down. I start to have symptoms of dehydration that seem to be bringing on another bad headache. Throughout the night, I am not able to leave the bathroom. My mom has me trying to drink fluids and observes me for any further symptoms of dehydration.

It is a week before Christmas, and I cannot believe I have the flu. I have a church Christmas play to prepare for, and there are kids counting on me to help them with their lines and costumes. Why is this happening now? I have always been the healthy child, and I rarely get the flu virus. Maybe this will be a twenty-four-hour flu and I will wake up tomorrow as my normal bubbly self.

It is December 20. I decide to continue to help the children at church with the Christmas play. As I head to practice, I can't seem to shake the cloudiness that is occupying my mind. I can't let the kids down; they are so excited and have put so much effort into preparing for this day.

All I can do is sit here. I am not able to focus, and the one line I have has escaped my mind. I have to leave. I feel like I am being strangled, and I need to get air. I will drive to my boyfriend Ricky's house. He will make me feel better.

I arrive, and I tell him, "I am so confused and have only had a few hours sleep in three days. And if I don't get to sleep soon, I am afraid my temper will get the best of me and I will lash out to my family and friends. And I don't want to hurt any of them, especially this time of year. How can I get sleep?" I ask him. "Just a few hours is all I need, and then I'll drive back home."

Ricky brings me a small blue pill, which is a psychiatric medication used to promote sleep. Trusting him, I decided to take it, not knowing anything about it or the side effects it can bring on. But I have to get some sleep before I start hallucinating.

The medication is effective in giving me a few hours of sleep, and I am able to drive home in the wee hours of the morning on December 21. I walk straight to my room, not wanting to disturb Mom or to confess to the medication I had ingested. Maybe insomnia is the reason I feel like this.

On December 21, my mom jumps up from a sound sleep at 4:30 a.m. to check on me. I walk into her room, and she was astonished by my appearance. My eyes were wide, and my pupils were dilated. I had a glazed look on my face, and all I could say was "Hi, Mom." My dad arrived home from work, and immediately, they knew something was wrong.

My parents asked me if I took any drugs. I did not other than sleeping medication, but I failed to mention this since I didn't know at the time the name of the medication, only that it did help me sleep for a few hours.

I immediately ran down the steps to the laundry room. I was followed by my mother, who was very concerned about my appearance and that when I spoke, I averted my gaze. The expression on my face, as told by my mom, was that there was a light on but that no one was home.

I ran to the dryer, opened up the door, and removed a sock from inside. I began pulling lint off the sock then grabbed another and again had to remove all the lint from it. I pulled out an article of clothing and pulled every little hair from the clothing. I then ran upstairs to the bowl of fruit in the kitchen and had to fix it to where each item was straight. My behavior was very bizarre.

I had psychomotor agitation and couldn't seem to relax. Was this from that one pill I took? Could it have been from the past weekend when I was partying with my friends? What was causing me to have these types of symptoms?

Perseveration

As the day progresses on December 21, I become more confused and continually play with my long blonde hair. Now my jaw seems to be moving uncontrollably. Mom notices this new symptom, which resembles patients exhibiting extrapyramidal symptoms.

Extrapyramidal symptoms are a group of side effects associated with antipsychotic medications and include parkinsonism, akathesia, dystonia, tardive dyskinesia, and bradyphrenia.

My mother is a psychiatric nurse and has heard of all these side effects related to these types of medications. They are involuntary movements that cannot be controlled or stopped by the individual experiencing them. The rest of my day consists of playing with my hair and displaying movements of my jaw resembling someone chewing food.

It is 11:00 p.m. on the twenty-first. As we are all trying to sleep, I again find myself sick to my stomach. I am unable to make it to the bathroom in time, and I remember telling my mom in a very slow tone, "It's everywhere."

"What is everywhere?" she asks.

I threw up, and it's everywhere. Mom immediately checks on me, and after helping me with my hygiene, she has me lie down to get some much needed rest.

I again tell her, "It's everywhere." And I tell her other things like I am going to be rich like Marilyn Monroe. These statements I repeat several times. This makes my parents significantly concerned; they are unsure if this is drug-related and will pass or if it's something neurological and I am experiencing perseveration.

Perseveration is the repeating of a word, phrase, or movement. This is what I have been doing lately by repeating phrases such as "It's everywhere" and "I will be rich like Marilyn Monroe." The constant playing with my hair also falls into this category.

It is December 22. I am quiet today. I seem to be taking longer in getting ready for church. My mom has to continually instruct me to perform my daily living skills.

"Hannah, brush your teeth and go get dressed. We are going to be late for church."

I stand speechless and motionless for several minutes. There seems to be a delay in processing the information that she is coaching me on.

My movements are slow; it takes me several minutes to put my boots on and even longer to tie them. I continue to have no appetite, but I seem to be relieved of the flu-like symptoms that I have exhibited recently.

I continue to have involuntary movements of my jaw as if I am constantly chewing on something. This continuous movement is causing me to have some of the most intense headaches I have ever experienced. My face is pale with a flat affect, and I continue to display poor eye contact. There seems to be a cloud interfering with my thoughts, but I need to help the children at church perform their play.

We arrive at church, and I continue to be very quiet, sitting with my parents and unable to assist the children with their performance. The director is looking for me to get up on stage and recite my line. This outgoing girl who has performed in numerous church plays and high school musicals did not know her cue or her line.

I stand on stage and continuously play with my hair and move my mouth as though I am chewing on a wad of gum. I was very quiet in saying my line. No one could hear me, and I am not sure if I even said it right. After I was done, I sat with my parents. I did not recognize many of the people in the congregation who I had known for years. It appears that I am in a new place with new faces, and I did not even understand the purpose of me being there.

After church, my mom prepared a delicious lunch for us, and we have our family time like we always do on a Sunday afternoon. My mom has always found it important to set aside one day during a hectic week where we can relax as a family and have some quality time and a home-cooked meal. She fixed my plate of food and placed it on the table.

"Hannah, come eat," she said.

I walk to the table and stare at my food for a brief moment then return to my bedroom. I sit on my bed and play with my hair.

Again, my mom yells at me to come and eat. And again, I just stare at my plate then return to my little corner on my bed. It was as if I didn't know what to do with that food. Or was it that I just wasn't hungry?

We are driving to the mall this afternoon for some last-minute Christmas shopping. Our list seems to grow longer every year. My mom is at the entrance of the mall and turns around to see me cleaning out the car and picking up every minute piece of paper off the floor. I cannot tolerate anything dirty or disorganized as it seemed to bring on anxiety.

After several minutes of my mom calling for me, I stopped my cleaning and went into the mall with her. This was something new for me as this had never bothered me in the past. I have always had a clean room, but it was cluttered with makeup and clothing that did not bother me if it was lying across my desk or on my bed. This behavior is worrying to my mom, but she believes that this too shall pass.

I continued to have a dull mood no matter how excited my mom tried to get me to be as we strolled through the mall and looked at the Christmas lights and displays. We have always enjoyed running to the mall at the last minute and observing others hurrying to pick up their last-minute gifts. I don't understand why this year I feel like there is no emotion in me and constantly feel numb.

This evening, Mom asks me to finish wrapping the gifts for our Christmas Eve celebration at my aunt's home, which is now only two days away. I pick up the wrapping paper and scissors and just hold them, not knowing what their function is. I have always loved to wrap gifts, and I always put so much time and effort into every little detail. I decided to go to my room and lie down as I felt another headache coming on.

Concerned because of my flat affect and the involuntary movement of my jaw, my parents transported me to a local hospital and informed the triage nurse that I was exhibiting a change in mental status. Prior to working as a psychiatric nurse, Mom worked in the emergency department and always received the phrase "Acute mental status change" as a high-priority complaint. The physician completed his assessment and ordered a CT scan, labs, and a urine drug screen test.

My parents know that I spend the weekends with my friends and are naïve to the fact that we have dabbled in different substances. It's hard for them to believe that their perfect little girl is not strong enough or even willing to say no. If the drug screen test comes back positive, I will feel that I have deeply disappointed them. My parents have always instilled Christian values into my siblings and I, but we make our own choices without thinking of the outcome.

As I wait for the results of the tests, I begin to repeat my words, laugh inappropriately, and cry. I do not understand why my emotions are fluctuating so quickly regardless of the situation. Could it be because of the stress of the holidays, my heavy schedule, and insomnia?

The doctor entered the room. He said unconcernedly, "The results of the CT scan are negative. The blood work revealed only a slight decrease in hemoglobin but not enough to justify iron supplementation." He then stated that the urine drug screen was unfounded but believes this is drug related and as the drug decreases in my body, I will return to my normal self.

My parents are relieved, and we can begin to look forward to Christmas, which is less than two days away.

December 23 brings another sleepless night with no improvement in my symptoms. I continue to have no appetite and spend most of the day isolating myself in my bedroom with no family interactions. My affect remains flat, and I continue to battle migraine headaches, which seem to never flee. I have lost that glow and joy that makes me who I am.

Evening brings our mother-and-daughter tradition to bake all our Christmas cookies in one night. My favorite is chocolate chip, which has made my mom very popular over the years in the eyes of her husband and children. I always look forward to this night of listening to Christmas music and wearing our festive aprons that display cute little female elves with spatulas in hand and cookies scattered all over the aprons. This cookie-baking marathon does not end until Christmas Eve morning.

This year, I cannot get myself motivated to help her bake. Is it due to the lack of sleep or my not knowing what to do with the ingredients? I start to develop severe nausea and a piercing headache and have to stay in bed. After a few minutes, I let out a terrifying scream and jumped from my bed. My parents quickly enter my room with looks of great concern and find me brushing myself off frantically as though I am covered in something. I see hundreds of ladybugs everywhere and crawling all over me.

I yell out, "Get them off me!"

My parents look around to find only a few ladybugs in the light fixture. Dad removes the light fixture and cleans it out, and Mom vacuums my room and changes my sheets. This is another new symptom that has my parents extremely concerned. Is this all related to insomnia? After all, there is evidence that shows lack of sleep can produce hallucinations.

On December 24, my parents are off to work for a few hours. Afterward, Mom will be purchasing items for our Christmas Eve party at my aunt Shirley's tonight. I find myself quiet today with breakthroughs of tearfulness for no apparent reason. I again remove items from the refrigerator without retuning them and strip my linens off my bed for fear that there are bugs in my sheets.

My sister Courtney decides to call Mom at work, concerned that I am getting worse and may have meningitis. Mom closes the door to her office and begins crying. How can her healthy, active perfect daughter succumb to any type of illness? And why would the other physician discharge me without concern?

"This is a nightmare," she thought. "It's Christmas Eve, and we are celebrating with family this evening. She is such a strong woman, but this must be too much for her to handle."

My parents decide to take me to the University of Pittsburgh Medical Center along with Ricky, who has been very supportive throughout this whole ordeal. We drive the forty-five minutes to Pittsburgh for a thorough evaluation by a nationally recognized hospital. En route I laugh inappropriately and begin repeating to Ricky that we are going to be rich like Marilyn Monroe. I am able to eat half a sandwich and drink some fluids. My parents are hopeful that they will find the cause and remedy it and that I'll be home just in time for Christmas.

In the emergency room, Mom gives the doctor a rundown on my health history, stressing that I have an acute change in mental status. While the physician is discussing my treatment, Mom begins talking about how when we return home she would be making Christmas lasagna. I began laughing uncontrollably; there was something about lasagna for Christmas that I thought was hysterical. Mom began laughing, which isn't something she has done for a while.

The physician walks into my room and proceeds to inform my parents that he is ordering a CT scan and blood work. Mom explains that I was seen two days ago at a local hospital and that the CT scan was negative. This physician ordered for this test to be repeated to ensure its accuracy. Labs were drawn. Now we just had to await the results to see where we go from here.

The results of the CT came back normal, and the labs were also within normal limits. My parents insisted on more testing and did not want me discharged without answers. While the doctors were contemplating treatment, my parents had to remove themselves to the waiting area. Again, my remarkably strong mom broke down in the waiting area in front of others. Dad calls Pastor Raul, who prays with them and tells them, "This too shall pass." My mom called a friend of mine, Shelly, to find out if I have been involved in drugs, what kind, and who was supplying them.

Shelly stated that there was a group of kids who have tried marijuana but would not give names. Mom was concerned that I may have had K2 spice laced with something that caused drug-induced schizophrenia. She is terrified that this brought on a temporary psychosis that will have a long recovery time. Mom asked Shelly if anyone else is exhibiting any of the symptoms I am having. Shelly stated that there haven't been any reports from the group of any illness.

My parents return to my room. Mom has a smile on her face so that I would not be frightened.

The doctor came back into the room and said, "Good news. The CT is negative."

"How is this good news?" Mom said sternly. "There is something going on, and you are missing it." Mom, who always tries to guard her words, was becoming increasingly irritated.

"A perfectly healthy, smart, and active girl does not have a change in mental status without reason. There is something happening, and you must find out what it is."

My parents insist that I be admitted for further evaluation consisting of a lumbar puncture, which would detect if there is an infection undetected in my body.

The doctors were reluctant, and my sister's friend, who is a doctor in Pittsburgh, persuaded them to perform the procedure. As each moment passes by, I am becoming more confused and disoriented. I am admitted to the eighth floor of UPMC for further testing. My parents are relieved that I am not being sent home and will have further care before being discharged home. Little did we know what the next several months would bring.

The only room at the inn is the cardiac floor. It has several elderly patients suffering from heart problems, which may not be a compatible placement for this girl. The view overlooking the city is breathtaking with the lights enhancing the beauty of the snowflakes falling intensely from the starlit sky on this Christmas Eve night.

I will lose the next couple of months of my life, and it will only be told to me by my family, evidenced by dramatic video and hospital documentation.

Mom tucks me in, hoping that I will get some much needed sleep. But my brain will not allow me. I feel as though I am jumping out of my skin. I am a caged animal that no one can control. I walk briskly and repeatedly from my bed to the bathroom with no purpose other than to move. I am experiencing what is referred to as psychomotor agitation.

I go into the bathroom, pull my pants up and down quickly, and then grab the faucet handle. I turn the water on and off, repeating this several times. I pick up my toothbrush and run it under the water several times then place it back down on the sink. This cycle occurs several times. I only stop to look at my mom, who is wrapped in a blanket and is sitting on the register. I tell her that she is always cold and that it's very annoying. She knew she could not stop me and that I had to perform these acts as my brain cannot be controlled.

Mom turned her head and looked up at the night sky. She is in disbelief at what is occurring. She prays to God to bring to light what is happening to her once bubbly child who always lights up a room but seems to have recently lost her sparkle.

My *parents drove home that evening to gather clothes and toiletries. The ride home was quiet, only broken by periods of crying from Mom. Ricky stayed with me and coaxed me to get some sleep, which is always an impossible feat. I felt warm, and he had the nurse check my temperature. I had a low-grade fever and was given a fever reducer.*

I tossed continuously and could not stop moving my legs. I continued to feel warm and restless without relief. Ricky asked the doctor to give me a sleeping pill. The nurse administered Ambien, which had no effect and was like taking a placebo. I was unable to keep any fluids down, so they decided it was time for intravenous fluids.

*When my parents arrived home, they placed me on the prayer chain. They have to rely on God through this storm that has caught all of us off guard and completely changed the lives of our family. My parents read an encouraging scripture in Isaiah (*NIV*) that says, "He gives strength to the weary and increases the power of the weak, even youth grow tired and weary and young men stumble and fall. But those whose hope is in the*

Lord will renew their strength, they will soar on wings like eagles, they will run and not grow weary they will walk and not be faint." This is a trying time for my family and has only just begun.

On December 25, my parents arrive early with our suitcases, which contain only a few items. We hope we will be leaving the hospital soon and can get back to our normal, everyday lives. Dad gives me a gift, and I immediately throw it across the room. I am disoriented to time and place, and I am unaware that this is Christmas Day. I jump out of bed and run back and forth from my bed to the bathroom. Mom follows me out of concern for my safety. I again turn the faucet on and off several times as though I have obsessive-compulsive disorder.

I eventually sit down on the commode, and as I am sitting here, I look to the right. My eyes are fixated on a sign that has a male cartoon character saying for me to wash my hands. I stare at the figure then point and say to Mom in a quiet, suspicious whisper, "That's him. He's the one who was staring at me through my bedroom window."

Mom notices how frightened I am and removes the picture from the wall and hides it in the bathroom cupboard. She is astonished by the symptoms I am experiencing. I am presenting signs of OCD, delusions, and paranoid schizophrenia. In all the years she has worked as a psychiatric nurse, she has only heard patients say they see or hear things but never has she witnessed it firsthand and from her own daughter, no less. Am I developing schizophrenia? Experts say this disease manifests in the early twenties and is uncommon in a healthy individual who is only seventeen and has no family history of mental illness other than anxiety disorder. Is this hitting me in the prime of my life and robbing from me my senior year of high school?

I return to my bed, sit in its center, and move my hands like that of a person who is crocheting and ask those around me, "Do you want to knit, honey? Come on, honey, let's knit a sweater." I then look into the air and begin talking about the millions of dust particles I see flying through the air. Why am I the only one who sees them? What is going on in my head that I want to knit and am obsessed with all these particles?

I continue to have a low-grade temperature of unknown origin and episodes of vomiting, and I seem to be losing weight rather quickly. The nurse brings me a pill to stop the nausea and continues to keep me hydrated. Mom begins playing my favorite song, and I begin to sing. But once the high note came, I screamed, causing the staff to run into my room. I continue to do this throughout the song. Mom places her hand over my mouth, hoping to mute my screams due to the fact this floor has cardiac patients and they do not need the added stress to their already compromised health.

Several residents come in and out of the room to take a peek at this unusual case that has everyone scratching their heads. I become agitated with all this traffic and strange people asking so many questions. I cannot tolerate too many people talking at once; it seems to overstimulate my brain, and all sounds are intensely magnified.

I jump out of bed with a terrified look on my face and run out to the nurse's station. I am looking for a quiet place to hide and attempt to go into another patient's room. The doctor on duty feared for the safety of the other patients and informed my dad that he must keep me under control or security will be called. I am amazed at the strength I possess at this time and how difficult it is for people to keep me under control. This quiet cardiac floor has been turned upside down by my arrival.

The physician working this evening has diagnosed me with insomnia and states that this will cause me to have delusions and hallucinations. She decides to write discharge papers and a prescription for Ambien. Is this really all it is? And can it be cured with a sleeping pill? My parents are hoping it's this easy and that I can be healed and finish out my senior year of high school.

As my parents were gathering up our belongings, a psychiatrist, Dr. Vint Blackburn, walks into the room this Christmas evening. After reviewing my puzzling history, he begins to speak with my parents. Little did we know that this is one of God's divine interventions.

Dr. Blackburn interviewed me, and with paucity and perseveration of speech, I respond, "I just need sleep. I just need sleep."

This girl who was recently in charge of fund-raising for choir could not even do a basic math calculation. I said to the psychiatrist, "I am scared." But I couldn't give the doctor any more information than that.

He speaks with my parents and informs them that my behavior shows that I am genuinely terrified and that this is not some teenage bravado. I place the blanket over my head, make only minimal eye contact, and become withdrawn and somnolent. I inform the doctor that there are voices in my head telling me to sleep.

Dr. Blackburn tells my parents he will not allow the other doctor to discharge me and will fight for me to have a medical work up to rule out an underlying medical illness that's manifesting as a psychiatric disease. Dr. Blackburn orders a test for synthetic cannabinoids as these do not test positive for marijuana. He is concerned that I may have ingested marijuana that was laced with a component that could have caused drug-induced schizophrenia. He also wants an MRI, EEG, TSH, NMDA panel and neuro consult to rule out encephalitis.

It is December 26. I have an EEG done and was not happy with all this glue and wires on my head; I can't help but scratch myself due to the intense itch it caused me. The neurologist asks me the days of the year, and I am unable to state them all. I am able to state my location, but I do not understand why I am here.

The neurologist reviews the lumbar puncture and states that it is consistent with a viral process. The MRI with contrast was unremarkable. The EEG showed generalized slowing with right temporal delta slowing. Findings of my exam are consistent with viral encephalitis HSV, but due to my frequent emesis, enterovirus is a possibility.

The final diagnosis was made: viral encephalitis. My parents are so relieved that we finally have a diagnosis and that this can be cured with antiviral medication. My mom is so excited that she cannot wait to get me home in time to shop for a gown for the winter ball.

The doctor on duty ordered Acyclovir IV; my mother had noticed as the IV was running, I began to get a diffuse body rash and became pink and itchy. I did not have a fever, but the rash was spreading. Mom asked the doctor to check to see if I was allergic to the medication. The doctor felt this was unlikely, but he stopped the infusion and consulted dermatology. By the time they arrived, the rash was gone. Was it an allergic reaction or viral exanthem? Did the virus leave my body and now I am cured?

The next day, my mom awakes with a great expectation that she will find me better from what acyclovir I did receive and that they we will be going home soon. I haven't seen my brother, Davey, in several days and want to catch up on school drama.

My symptoms have grown more severe, and my mental status continues to deteriorate. My dad asks the physician if whatever is going on in my body could be the result of a sinus infection that I had a couple weeks ago. Could this infection have spread to my brain? Dad also shared with the doctor that before we came to the hospital, it took me ten minutes to put my socks on. Currently, it seems like everyone and everything is moving in slow motion and that this may be causing me to speak in slow motion.

Work up this far has included LP, MRI, several EEGs, and acyclovir. I continue to baffle the medical field with the doctor having my parents sign a release to do a case study on me to publish. A case study? This can't be good. My parents are living the scripture in Thessalonians where you pray without ceasing.

At baseline, the physician documents how energetic and involved I am in activities at school and in the community. What can cause someone like me to suddenly develop such an acute mental status change with no significant prior medical history?

The doctor questions my dad if I have farm animals, traveled outside the United States, or have recently been camping, all to which my dad answers no. The dermatologists could not find any tick bites on my skin or any other skin lesions.

It is December 29, 2013. My medication cocktail arrives consisting of Benadryl, Ativan, Toradol, and Zofran. I think they are trying to keep this girl calm until they find out what is going on. I have been rather agitated and sarcastic and have never had an attitude like this. I cannot seem to control my reactions or filter my words. I hope that everyone understands and that I don't hurt anyone as a result.

I have lost my orientation to time the clock, and the current date has no relevance. I continue to be oriented to person and place, for now. The EEG cart comes in again, and the wires are all attached. I become combative and stand up on the bed and become entangled in the IV tubing and wires. Security is called, and the nurse places a medication in my IV to help me to relax. I peer out my hospital room door and find two security guards standing by.

The viral studies came back, and they were all negative for EBV, CMV, HSV, and VZV. Due to no improvement in my condition, further work up will be ordered. The doctors were holding on to a viral etiology, but they now realize that there is another causative agent. They will be holding a conference to discuss the next step.

The physicians agreed that due to me being just seventeen years old, I go under pediatrics; thus, they are transferring me to the children's hospital in Pittsburgh. Will I have to go through all these tests again? My parents inform my family, and my grandfather asks Pastor Dean Blythe of Hopedale Church of Christ and the wonderful congregants to pray that a diagnosis is soon discovered and that God gives us the strength to endure what lies ahead.

On December 30, I arrive at the children's hospital, and my parents start running down my recent history yet again.

I am a little weaker and have a hard time standing up to ambulate to the bathroom. I take a sip of water from my mom and then spit it out all over her and begin to blow foamy spit bubbles and wouldn't stop. The resident ordered me NPO since it looked to her that I had trouble swallowing. My mom was not happy as she has been constantly trying to get fluids and bites of food in me.

A swallow evaluation was done and unfounded; my mother was thrilled when she was able to give me sips of water. The neurology team arrives, and they ask me where I am. I state that I am in Toronto, Ohio. Now I am not even aware of the place. Will I soon forget who I am? The neurologist then asks me to move my leg. I respond and continue to move my leg even after he says to stop. I then begin thrashing in bed and rolling in bed. I cannot lie still. I begin to have hyperventilation and periods of crying and laughing. My brain is so irritated, but why?

I continue to have this need to move around in bed. My dad asks the nurse to help me to relax in the fear that I am going to hurt myself. Nothing seems to help slow my mind down. More EEGs are ordered, this one for twenty-four hours to see if there are any subtle seizures that can be detected. I have recently been checked for Lyme's disease, which came back negative, and the physicians ruled out vector-borne encephalitis. A thyroid level was also done due to the fact that hyperthyroidism or thyrotoxicosis could bring about psychiatric symptoms such as anxiety and labile mood as well as psychosis. The results were negative, only making this situation more difficult to conclude.

Neurology again assesses me and reveals worsening of confusion and disorientation. Stat MRI, EEG, and LP is ordered. EEG is abnormal but shows no seizure activity, and the MRI is normal. LP shows eight white blood cells. The team continues to think it is a viral encephalopathy.

My parents take videos of me as requested by the neurologists so that they can monitor my behavior and involuntary muscle movements to try to pull everything together. My parents are meeting with dozens of neurologists, some present and others via telemedicine, to ask my parents questions on my prodromal symptoms. The head of neurology has me appearing on a large screen to have everyone see my behavior and the symptoms I am exhibiting. They are looking at my cognitive function in responding to commands. This once perfectly groomed girl is now disheveled in appearance and not responding appropriately to commands. I am thankful that even in my sickness, I am able to teach others who will be caring for those who succumb to this cruel illness that wants to rob its victims of two months of their lives that will never be restored. My parents continue in the faith and believe that Jesus has a plan and a purpose for my madness.

More blood tests are completed to check for cat scratch fever and HIV, both of which return with negative results. More labs are sent to the Mayo Clinic in Rochester,

Minnesota to check for a rare condition that affects the NMDA receptors in the brain. This test will require three days for the results, and my parents are growing more eager for the doctors to find the diagnosis. Not knowing what is going on with me is hard for them, but they continue to be two of the strongest people I know. Back home, the community is forming fund-raisers for my family, with prayer vigils being held in our sister churches in Puerto Rico, Honduras, and Miami.

It is important when battling any illness to have a strong support system by your side and those who are dedicated to prayer. My family has been with me the whole time; if my parents are at work, my aunt Lori sits with me.

My mouth opens like I want to speak, but no sounds are made and it appears to be in a frozen state. I cannot close it on my own and seem to be experiencing catatonia and will be given high doses of benzodiazepines to counteract it. Mom has to physically close my mouth for me.

The neurologist lifts my left arm to check muscle strength, and my arm remains in that position, a term called waxy flexibility. It remains this way until someone puts it down. If I had a torch in my hand, I would resemble the Statue of Liberty. The psychiatric team comes in and tries to convince mom that I need ECT treatments to come out of catatonia. Mom tells the team that she does not believe ECT should be given to those afflicted with encephalitis. She feels the brain is too fragile with this illness and this treatment could lead to more damage than good. The team approaches her several more times throughout my ordeal with catatonia, and every time, Mom refuses.

I am unable to follow direct commands and continue to grow increasingly weak. My Babinski reflexes are minimal, which is a sign of neurological decline. A few short months ago, I was heading up a fund-raiser for choir and in charge of the money. Now I cannot even perform the simplest of calculations or count backward. Cognitively, I have severely declined.

New Year's Eve 2013

Mom is sitting by the window. She is staring down at the busy streets of Pittsburgh and thinking about all those who are getting ready to celebrate with family and friends in all their glittery attire and anticipating the arrival of the new year.

Normally, I would be getting dressed in a sequined outfit and have my hair and makeup done. I would then go to a romantic dinner with Ricky and then attend several parties with our friends. I never could have imagined this is where I would be on New Year's Eve.

Mom sits by the window. She looks toward heaven and wonders whether I will see this New Year and, if so, if I will be cognitively impaired. It is still hard for her to believe that this is even happening. She continues to hold on to her faith and begins reading Ecclesiastes 3:1 (KJV), "To everything there is a season and a time to every purpose under the Heaven," and Jeremiah 29:11 (NIV), "For I know the plans I have for you declares the Lord. Plans to prosper you and not to harm you, plans to give you a hope and a future." Mom truly believes that trials strengthen and equip us with a strong testimony that will encourage others and that Jesus has a plan and purpose for this season in our lives.

How do people even survive times like these without Jesus as their strong tower? This could be traumatizing and discouraging and create feelings of despair and depression. He is our hope and our comforter.

New Year's Day 2014

TYPICALLY, I WOULD be setting our large oak table with Mom's best dishes for the arrival of our New Year's Day guests. I place daffodils in the center of the table; these flowers represent rebirth and new beginnings. Mom makes her pork and sauerkraut with baked apples and cranberries. I, being the excellent baker that I am, make a homemade cherry cheesecake and Davey's favorite dessert, which is chocolate fudge cake drenched in peanut butter icing. Mawmaw brings her famous macaroni salad and Nana her dressing.

We watch the New Year's Day parade and a recording of football, which is usually the Dallas Cowboys. They are, by the way, my uncle Steve's favorite team and with whom Mom, in her younger years, was asked by the organization to try out for cheering. This is one of our favorite times to sit and relax with family and friends, but the harsh reality is that I am stuck in this hospital bed. I am growing weaker at each passing moment, and now, I cannot walk, talk, or eat. I do not have the strength to open my eyes to the world around me.

Mama turns and positions me frequently to prevent ulcers from forming on my delicate skin, and Dad moves my legs every fifteen minutes to prevent deep vein thrombosis, also known as blood clots. They start me on Lovenox injections to help as well, and before long, my abdomen is covered in bruises. I'm sure that if I could come out of this unconscious state and open my eyes to gaze upon their faces, I would see two people who are the picture of complete exhaustion but who still seem to find the strength and capabilities to endure.

I can't help but feel responsible for Mom's weight loss. She doesn't eat much because I am unable to eat and she feels too guilty. But she understands the importance of keeping her strength and stamina up to be able to care for me. Mom constantly looks at the monitor to check my vitals and heart rhythm. My oxygen saturation is also being monitored, and oxygen is readily available if needed. My legs and feet feel cool due to decreased circulation, so Dad applies warm socks and a wool blanket.

The next morning, the neurologist, Dr. Alper, bursts into the room carrying the lab results. "We have a diagnosis," she says.

My parents jump to their feet; this is the moment they have been praying for. She opens the manila envelope and reads the information to us.

"Your daughter has anti-NMDA receptor encephalitis. This is an acute form of encephalitis that is caused by an autoimmune reaction to NMDA receptors in the brain. Her own body is attacking the proteins located in her brain and sees them as a foreign invader. This is a newly discovered disease that requires so much more information on etiology, treatments, and prognosis. We know that it can be genetic. Do you have any family members with autoimmune disorders?"

Dad proceeds to tell Dr. Alper that we have a cousin with rheumatoid arthritis and a great-aunt with lupus.

The prodromal signs are headaches, flu-like symptoms, and an upper respiratory infection, all of which I experienced before this disease hit its peak. The behavioral changes come next such as anxiety, confusion, insomnia, grandiose delusions, fear, mania, paranoia, and psychosis. Bizarre movements of the mouth and lips can occur, which I have exhibited. I looked like Elvis Presley with one side of my mouth drawn upward.

Elvis is my Mawmaw's favorite singer, and she has several memorabilia of Elvis and a picture of Graceland. One of her favorite songs is "Walking in Memphis" since this is about Elvis and his hometown. I have never been to Memphis and may never have the opportunity to visit, but I enjoy looking at all the pictures she has in her album.

My parents are relieved that we finally have a diagnosis, and Dr. Alper inform them that treatment can begin immediately.

"What are the treatments for this disease?" Dad asks.

The first line treatments are steroids and immunoglobulin. The purpose of immunoglobulin is to suppress immunity, more specifically the NMDA receptor antibody, so she will stop producing antibodies that attack the brain. The bag of immunoglobulin, the first of five, drips slowly into my delicate veins accompanied by high-dose steroids. My parents screen any visitors before they are authorized to enter my room for fear I will obtain a secondary infection due to my decreased immune system.

I continue to remain in an unconscious state and now require placement of a nasogastric tube for nutritional supplementation. I'm sure that if I was awake this tube would not be in for long. The physicians continue to monitor my condition to observe for any improvement with the first line treatments. We are all hoping that this is all I will need and that in a few days I will be able to return home. I have so much I need to accomplish this year, and I feel like people are depending on me to help organize fund-raisers, assist in yearbook production, and perform in this year's musical.

I will be sent for a CT scan to check for teratomas, which are ovarian tumors that are one cause of this disease. About 80 percent of individuals who have this are females, and approximately half have a teratoma. I believe Mom is praying for a tumor so it can be removed and the recovery time will be hastened with less chance of relapse. Mom believes that God is not a god of relapse and that once I am healed I will be healed to completion.

I, on the other hand, will be delighted if I do not have a tumor. I have always dreamed of getting married and having two children, one boy and one girl. Children have a special place in my heart, especially those who are ill or have developmental disorders. God has created each one of us with a specific purpose and plan, and all have great value and significance: "For you formed my inward parts and wove me in my mother's womb" (Ps. 139:13, NASB). I hope to one day be able to share my story, to be an example of strength and hope, and to encourage others who are sick to continue to fight and to glow after the darkness.

My CT scan is completed, and my parents anxiously await the results. The steroids I am receiving are significantly raising my blood sugar, and they have hypoglycemic agents on standby if the change in nutrition is not effective in lowering my glucose.

Before I became ill, we had a little boy in our community who was newly diagnosed with leukemia. His name is Noah. We held a fund-raiser for him and sold T-shirts that said "Noah's Warriors." He is an excellent artist and walks closely with Jesus. His family is strong and also has much community support. Little did I know that he would be one floor below me and that we would be fighting our battles together.

No one should have to fight cancer, especially children. My family has several members who have cancer or who are currently diagnosed. This is another cruel illness that wants to take away the quality and quantity of life. I hope someday to be able to visit children with cancer to encourage them to never give up and to remain strong.

The CT scan came back negative for ovarian tumors. Mom tells the radiologist that she believes they missed something; Mom doesn't want to face the reality that I may need further treatment. She is hoping for a quick recovery and to avoid the second-line treatments that are just on the horizon.

I am becoming more autonomically unstable, with my blood pressure and pulse fluctuating from very high to very low and my body unable to regulate my temperature. I continue to have a fever that they are struggling to combat. This is the critical part of the illness, and there are some who do not recover from this. I am having breathing irregularities ranging from hyperventilation to hypoventilation. The doctor is watching to see if I need to be intubated.

Because I am unstable, they are transferring me to the pediatric intensive care unit and will begin the second-line treatment consisting of plasmapheresis. In plasmapheresis, they will insert a catheter into my jugular vein and remove my own plasma and replace it with donor plasma. This has its own risks, but my parents know that I am gravely ill and have no choice but to agree to this procedure.

It's ironic that my youth leader would be outside working on the machine that could save my life. Dad greets him out in the hallway and invites him in to see me, but he couldn't. He was afraid of what he would see and that it might be too hard for him to handle. He is always a jokester and enjoys making people laugh, but when it comes to sick children, it is something he doesn't understand. He walks away, trying to hold back the tears.

After several days of being in the PICU and receiving plasmapheresis, I was moved to another floor to be monitored. I continue to be unresponsive, and everyone is concerned because I have not shown any signs of improvement. Mom limits visitors; she does not want too many people seeing me in this current situation. I miss Davey, Courtney, and our Chihuahua, Daisee Mae. She always wags her tail and welcomes me when I come home from school.

The nurse comes into my room and administers potassium as my electrolytes are off balance. She shares with mom how she is going to rent a movie for her and her daughter and how they are going to stay up late and eat popcorn and ice cream. It is very inconsiderate, considering that I am unconscious; she might as well have stuck a knife in my mother's chest.

Mom made it a point to tell others not to take their children for granted and to enjoy the mundane because at any moment, life can change in the blink of an eye. How she longs to sit and talk with me over a bowl of cereal and see my smile. She misses my sweet voice and the ability to gaze into my beautiful blue eyes.

The next morning, while Mom is at work, Dad calls her to inform her that my vital signs have plummeted and that I am unresponsive. The doctor has to perform a sternal rub several times and is able to finally arouse me out of my comalike state. Mom immediately calls Pastor Raul and Deneen and could hardly speak through the tears. They immediately pray. Dad is deeply concerned with the length of time it took to wake me up. I finally start breathing adequately and have a bruise on my sternum from the effort of the physician. They quickly administer IV fluids in an attempt to raise my blood pressure.

Mom drives an hour from work back to the hospital. During the commute she asks God to please give her a sign that I will be okay. She is a woman of faith, but she realizes that there are times when we need God to show us that he has this. He wants us to talk with him just like an earthly father wants to talk with his children. Mom immediately receives a phone call from a lady she has never met. Her name is Brooke, and she tells my mom, "Don't worry. She will be okay." It was as though Jesus himself was talking through her because that is what she needed to hear.

She had a peace that passes all understanding and cried tears of gratitude before God and thanked him for that confirmation. He is faithful and will bring us a peace and comfort maybe in the form of someone else. He is not walking with my parents during this time; he is carrying them.

My vital signs recover and become stable. My parents are on an emotional roller coaster, but they continue to do what most people cannot, and that is to comfort people who are in a crisis while they are going through their own. They certainly show others that you cannot only praise Jesus when you are on the mountaintop because the true test of faith is to praise him in the valley.

The immunoglobulin, high-dose steroids, and plasmapheresis have shown little improvement in my symptoms. The next treatment will be the use of Rituximab, which is a medication used in the treatment of cancer. Again, it is ironic how I have a heart for kids who have cancer but that I have to undergo chemotherapy and constantly deal with the nauseating effects and decreased immunity.

My parents read through the adverse reactions that can occur, but again, they have no choice but to let me receive the life-saving treatment. The medication is administered through my IV and will be the last treatment for this condition. I am starting to develop muscle breakdown, especially in my calves. The physical therapist has to work with my legs even in my unconscious state.

January 17, 2014

I CONTINUE TO be unresponsive, not knowing what is taking place in the outside world. My church is having a spaghetti dinner for me. Hundreds will show up to show their support, and the church is filled to maximum capacity. My parents are overwhelmed with the support. I didn't realize how many people actually cared. When it comes to giving a helping hand, Toronto delivers.

Our local news team, News 9, is there interviewing my parents to update everyone on my condition. My dad has prayed numerous times for a News 9 worthy move of God in Toronto, and little did he know that his daughter would be the topic.

Mom invited Brooke and was able to meet her and thank her for calling that day she was driving to the hospital and needed confirmation that I would be okay. Brooke also shared her story of healing, and everyone seemed to be touched by what God is doing.

This winter so far has been one of the worst with the amount of snowfall, and still people came out and made the dinner a huge success. My classmates sold "Our Queen is a fighter" T-shirts in my favorite pink and black colors. So many people have been involved that it's impossible to thank them all.

January 2014

A PRAYER VIGIL is being held at the gazebo in the middle of town; it is hosted by my musical family. I know I will have to give up my role as Belle. I have waited for the lead role for several years, and when I finally get the lead in my senior year, I cannot participate. I have to believe that God has bigger and better plans. His ways are not our ways.

Dozens are gathered this frigid January evening to pray for me. Mom made the trip back to pray and to thank everyone for coming out to pray. She shares with everyone that I continue to be unresponsive and require tube feedings for my nutrition. I continue to lose weight and my vitals fluctuate at times, but we are hopeful for a complete recovery.

Pastors, the musical director, and the superintendent of our schools all share scripture and pray for Noah and myself. Noah is our hometown hero and continues to be strong in his fight against leukemia. We don't understand why things happen, but we know that in every situation, we need to glorify God and trust that he is in control.

I will miss the band formal dance this year and have looked forward to every dance. I hope to make my senior prom in April. I dream of wearing a long white gown with silver embellishments on the bodice with a hoop underneath to make it full. We will see what the next couple of months bring.

February 2, 2014

I CONTINUE TO be unresponsive. My sister brings a CD player and plays Taylor Swift's *Red*. I open my eyes and begin looking around the room. I move my mouth to the words even though no sound comes out. Music has always been a big part of my life, and she is one of my favorite artists. The power of prayer and music seems to have brought me out of a catatonic state. Mom has a video of me moving my mouth to the words.

At this point, I still cannot move my extremities, but they are thrilled that I am awake. My family is overjoyed, and we are all singing today, even my mama who says she cannot carry a tune. She finally gets to look into my blue eyes once again.

The doctor says that they have exhausted all treatments and that we just have to allow the brain to heal, which could take up to two years. I am being transferred to the children's institute in Pittsburgh where I will undergo physical, speech, and occupational therapies. I will have to learn how to walk, talk, and eat. That was Mom's favorite saying to me: "Hannah, if you want to get better, you have to walk, talk, and eat."

I arrive at the children's institute. I am able to open my eyes, but I cannot speak. My body is stiff and rigid. The nurse wants to give me a shower; I have had only sponge baths for almost two months. The nurse, Mom, and Dad stand in a line and scoop me up then pivot to place me onto the shower table.

Before I left the hospital, they surgically placed a gastric tube into my stomach, which will be easier on my liver than the N/G tube feedings. Mom stays by my bedside, and Dad sleeps at the Heasley House right next door and is a blessing for families with children in the institute.

Every morning, my parents wake up hoping to find me completely healed. I continue to take high doses of benzodiazepines and steroids. I also continue the Lovenox injections to prevent blood clots. My stomach looks horrible with a gastric tube protruding from it, and I have several bruises due to the shots. I have an elevated temperature, and I am given high-dose antibiotics.

The antibiotics are causing bowel issues, and a sample is sent to the lab to check for clostridium difficile. Fluids run continuously, and I am starting to break down in my coccyx region. The results are negative for C-diff, and Mom frequently changes my position.

February 28, 2014

MOM IS READY to leave for work. She drives for an hour, works until five, and then drives an hour back though it is usually much longer with rush hour. God directed her path in nursing to help those inflicted with mental illness and substance abuse. It has to be difficult to help them with their problems and give them hope and peace when she is going through her own storm.

She gives me a kiss and asks God to give her another sign that I will be okay. She asks him to allow me to say Jesus. She hasn't heard me speak in about a month, and she longs to hear my sweet voice no matter how faint in tone it may be. She said, "Hannah, say Jesus." And again, she repeated it.

All of a sudden, in a clear and strong tone, I said, "Jesus." Mom began praising and thanking God. Mom called everyone to tell them that I had said my first word in a long while.

March 3, 2014

MOM AND I are sleeping, she in a very uncomfortable lounge chair and me in my hospital bed with erect rails. For some reason, Mom woke up and turned to check on me. She couldn't believe her eyes. Somehow, I was outside of my bed and hanging onto the rail for dear life. I didn't make a sound, and I have no idea how I managed to do this.

Mom is so excited. I haven't moved in a couple of months. Even though I was frozen in that spot and was waiting for mom to attempt to maneuver me back into bed, I moved. She's trying to get me back into bed before the nurse comes in and gets upset that I am on the floor. We are successful, and she tucks me back in bed to get some rest.

I have a long way to go on my journey, but we take it one moment at a time and trust in the Lord that this season in our lives will be over soon. Several weeks ago, God spoke a word to my dad that this is a difficult season but that spring is right around the corner. When we go through difficult circumstances, we need to remember that it is only temporary and that we need to hold on, persevere, and never give up.

A very encouraging scripture for this time of our lives and for anyone who finds that they are in a gloomy situation and wants to throw the towel in is Psalm 30:5 (NKJV), which states, "Weeping may endure for a night, but joy comes in the morning."

Mom will never forget the next day. This is a beginning of events that she has read about and heard about but has never truly witnessed. We feel as though the worst is behind us, but this illness is proving to be quite unpredictable.

A male employee, short in stature with only random tufts of hair, walks briskly back and forth while cleaning the room. With a genuine astonished look on my face, I pointed to the man walking back and forth quickly across the room and said, "Look at the monkey! Look at the monkey!" This shocked Mom, as she knew I had a genuine hallucination. In my mind, this person was a monkey.

The wonderful thing about this floor is that no matter what is said or done, they all understand that each one of us is suffering from trauma to our brain, be it from a head injury or encephalitis, and that we cannot control our thoughts and actions.

The brain, which weighs only three pounds, is so fascinating, and we only know very little about how it works. Mom witnessed this hallucination and gave her more of an appreciation for psychosis and those suffering from schizophrenia. No one can ever tell Mom that it doesn't exist because she will tell you otherwise.

March 14, 2014

WITH EACH PASSING day, I am growing a little stronger and am able to move a little more. I continue to have a decreased appetite and have nutrition through the gastric tube. This morning brings its own miracle. Today, the unimaginable happens. With deep exhaustion and a weak voice, I rose from my silence and opened into a beautiful melody that came from deep within my heart. My family is present to hear this, and they know that this is directly to my Savior and my Healer.

I begin to sing, word for word in its entirety, "Amazing Grace." My family, weeping, witnessed the most beautiful and heavenly sound. Everyone's faith grew this day, and my faith gives him the battle and me the victory. I realize that this time in my life will bring him glory. Our trials prove that we need a deliverer and that we cannot overcome on our own.

When I am better, I hope to sing with my dad on the worship team. The first song would be "Amazing Grace." God is showing me that in my weakness he is strong and that I need to rely on him and I can soar through any storm like the eagle. You see, the eagle is not afraid of the storm and is the only bird who will not fly around it or who is intimidated by it. The eagle flies directly into the storm.

The next morning, I begin all my therapies. But I am not a morning person. I am irritable and do not want to attend speech therapy. I have difficulty standing and require assistance to get on the wheelchair. I never dreamed I would need to rely on a wheelchair for transportation. A staff member applies my foot rests, and I attempt to kick them for being in my space.

Mom wheels me to see Dr. Sue, but in my illness, I call her Dr. Soup. She will be working with me to teach me to read and write. She gives me a spoon to see how my motor skills are. I take the spoon and the pudding and throw them at her and start grabbing things within my reach. I have to return to my room due to my agitation.

I lie down in bed. A few minutes later, Leslie, the occupational therapist, arrives. She takes me to the computer room and shows me prom gowns. She knows prom is in April and I am hoping to attend. I grab the computer and try to throw the monitor. Leslie intercepts it, and again, my lesson is cut short.

My physical therapist, Laura, arrives. I had built a close relationship with her and had begun to trust her. She takes me to the exercise room, where I sit in a chair and try to lift weights with my legs. Both my calves are weakened from the months of being bedridden, and they have slightly atrophied. This will be my routine every day until I improve.

I am starting to eat a little pureed food, but I am unable to hold the spoon. Mom probably thought she would never have to feed me and change me at this stage in my life. I attend physical therapy and walk six steps today. Mom is so excited with them, more than she was with my first baby steps. I am slowly getting stronger, but I am increasingly becoming agitated. It could be a combination of the encephalitis and the high-dose steroids.

I had always taken pride in my looks. Now my hair is thinning, and I have the moon-shaped face that comes with steroids. I head to OT, and Leslie is showing me graduation gowns. I am set to graduate on June 6. Mom is looking forward to me walking across the stage to get my diploma. Again, I am not interested in anything that Leslie has to show me, and I begin cursing. The staff members here are not offended; they truly understand what we are encountering.

Mom wheels me down to the game room to see if I want to borrow a movie. There are several people in there, and immediately, I need to retreat back to my room. I tell her they do not like me and that they are staring and talking about me. She takes me back to the room, where I feel safe.

I am able to speak more and begin ambulating in a stand-up walker; Laura takes me around the perimeter of the nurse's station. I begin to grab at everything within my reach, and they have to hold my arms down. I ambulate past an eighteen-year-old boy's room; the boy is cursing and combative. He was perfectly healthy until he was a passenger in an automobile that crashed into a tree. He is blind with severe brain damage. The driver was his girlfriend.

We must count our blessings daily and be thankful for our health and for our family. Life can change in the blink of an eye, be it from a tragic accident or encephalitis. I know my family's perspective has changed on what is truly important. It is not material things but the relationships we have with others that is going to be remembered.

I have music today with Haley. I love to sing. It has been my passion for as long as I can remember. Haley plays the guitar, and we sing together. But in the middle of the song, I begin to cry. I'm not sure if it's because I have missed singing or I think I will never have the same beautiful voice that I did before I became sick.

Haley attempts to sing a few songs with me, and one of them is "Blessings" by Laura Story. This is the song I sang for my Mawmaw in church when she was going through breast cancer. This is one of my favorite songs, and it talks about how are trials are his mercies in disguise and how they cause us to draw near to him.

I look forward to music therapy with Haley. During this time, it gives me an internal peace and takes away my irritability and anxiety. We also have things in common.

She has blonde hair, loves to sing, and was homecoming queen of her school.

I am in speech therapy, and Dr. Soup has me naming pictures. She shows me a picture of a bulldozer and asks me what it is. I cannot think of the name and call it a "big yellow chomp chomp thing." She shows me a picture of a foot, and I do not say "foot"; I say "pedicure." She asks me to read, and I refuse. Is it because I am irritable and stubborn? Or do I really not know how to read? My aunt Lori is with me, and she witnesses that I am not reading for Dr. Soup.

Aunt Lori takes me back to my room, and I lie down to rest. As I am lying there, I look up to the TV, and she has Fox News on. I begin to read all the headlines that quickly scroll at the bottom of the screen. Aunt Lori is amazed because she thought I wasn't able to read, and she chuckles at my devious behavior.

She sits with me, and we color and watch movies. Mom bought the newly released *Frozen* movie, and Aunt Lori and I watch it over and over again. I would have her sing "Let It Go" with me. My voice is getting stronger, and I hope to be singing in church again soon. Mom also brought in *Beauty and the Beast*, but it's Mom who can't watch it. She thinks about my missing out on the musical this year, and it does hurt. She is only human and tries not to let what I'm missing get to her, but it's difficult at times. She knows that God's grace in my life is enough.

I receive several cards and letters from friends, family, and my high school teachers. I also receive cards from people I do not even know. The support that has been shown is overwhelming; I am usually the one heading up fund-raisers and mailing get-well-soon cards.

Mom decorates the room with cards, homecoming pictures, and a handmade quilt that has my senior pictures on it. I had my senior pictures done at the end of September, not knowing what would be happening to me in just a few short months. The quilt is covered in signatures and get-well-soon wishes from my friends at church.

There are several fund-raisers being held back home. Heavenly bodies, Toronto Lanes, and Cornerstone Church, who is holding a spaghetti dinner. It's humbling and appreciated knowing so many people are thinking about me. My friend Ryan, who has autism, sent me a card; this truly is special to me.

It would be terrible thinking everyone has forgotten about you or that your life has no significance. I pray that when I am better, I can talk to others and tell them the value of their lives and how God sees them. He made each one as his masterpiece and places great value on each one. I love the particular scripture that says that he is no respecter of persons. He loves each one in the same way.

I'm walking on my own now; Laura has me trying to jump on a little trampoline to strengthen my calves. I am unable to do this and become unsteady. I used to be able to do flips and jump so high, but I need to be patient. I know that one day it will happen, but I am not calm and become more aggressive and agitated. I curse at Mom and Dad without remorse. This is not me; I have always had a gentle loving spirit.

Leslie walks me to occupational therapy to do one of my favorite things: baking. I become angry with Leslie and want to go to my room. She hands me the package of cake mix flour, and I immediately throw it on the ground and jump on it. Needless to say, chocolate flour went all over the kitchen. I then walked back to my room.

Supper arrives, and I refuse to eat. I look at the food then look at Mom and tell her, "They are trying to poison me." Mom reassures me the food is fine, but I don't believe her and know without a doubt that they are out to harm me. I go to bed, throwing the sheets over my head and peeking through to see if they are coming after me.

Mom sits and listens to that song again, "I Heard the Bells on Christmas Eve." Somehow, she finds solace in it.

I stare at my belly and yell, "I have aliens in there," wanting Mom to take them out. I begin to pull on my G-tube in an attempt to set them free. Mom sits next to me to make sure I don't pull it out.

I head to speech therapy and do reading comprehension with Dr. Soup. She is reading a story about Buzz Aldrin and how he was the second person to walk on the moon. She finishes reading it and asks me who the main character is, and I answer, "Buzz Lightyear." Mom starts to laugh, and then I laugh in a sarcastic manner.

She gives me paper and a pen, and I scribble and throw it back at her. I return to my room and begin yelling at Mom and cursing. I talk about Emma, a girl who was a friend of mine in school but how we were always in competition and she was very jealous of me.

I looked at Mom's face and said, "You are not my mom. You are Emma! I then try to hit her several times until she bear-hugs me. She puts me on the bed until I calm down.

Just then, the nurse walks in to give me nutrition through my tube. When she leans over, I try to punch her in the stomach. This nurse is several months pregnant, and I intentionally try to hit her. I refuse to answer questions and will repeat every word spoken by others in a sarcastic manner

This evening, Mom has the Bible, and I grab it from her and start reading it. I am fearful I have a demon and will be thrown into the lake of fire. I pray to Jesus and read out loud for an hour, even stating the punctuations as I read. I become tearful and ask my parents to pray for me.

The next day, I have episodes of combativeness with the staff and with Mom. She will play music to calm me down, which only works temporarily, and then I become angry again. Again, I look into her eyes thinking she is someone else and ask her, "What did you do with my mom?" And I begin to hit her. She calms me down and hands me the

Bible. I begin to read it, and Mom looks over to see what book I am reading.

I am reading the book of Mark. Mom is inquisitive as to why I am reading Mark. She sees my finger pointing to Mark 5:21–43. Jesus heals the woman with the issue of blood, and then what I read next brings tears to her eyes. Jesus took the little girl's hand and said, "Little girl, get up." And she was healed. Mom believes this is a word from the Lord to bring comfort and to confirm that I will be okay.

I then turn the page and rip it. I start crying and believe I am going to hell. Mom grabs the tape and tries to fix it. She tries to convince me that I will not go to hell. I cover my head to get some much-needed rest. I sleep for only a few moments and throw the sheets off; they are covered in dirt, and I will not sleep until the nurses get me clean linens. Mom gives me a reality orientation, which doesn't help because this is my reality.

Sunday morning is here, and Mom and I attend the church service here at the institute with the other children, several of whom have developmental delays or have been in accidents with severe brain injury. We begin singing, and I look at each one of them with a sincere compassion and caring heart. I ask God to help them and their families to remain strong and to never stop fighting.

I enjoy the music and the scriptures, but my heart is heavy and I ask Mom to take me back to my room and to never take me back there. It was too overwhelming to see so many kids going through illnesses and injuries. On the way to my room, we stopped by the lounge. Again, I cannot stay; everyone is staring at me, laughing, and calling me a freak. I begin to panic and walk quickly back to my room. The nurse brings me lunch, and I continue to think they are trying to poison me and refuse to eat.

Later that evening, I jump out of my bed and put my back against the wall, sliding across the room and looking side to side as though I am in an action movie and someone is out to get me. Mom is amazed at what the brain does when it is affected by trauma. She is witnessing a true form of paranoid schizophrenia, and she can't believe how cruel this illness is and the internal torture it causes those afflicted with it.

The next day, I awake and find Dad sitting at my bedside. I immediately look at him and say, "I hate you" and give him such an evil look. He hands me a carton of chocolate milk, and I take it and decide to dump it all over the floor, shaking it to get every drop out of it.

Dad has visitors in today. With them and the staff around, I am overwhelmed with noise and become very agitated. I cannot tolerate too many voices at once; it seems to overstimulate my brain. The IV starts beeping; it's all so magnified in my head, and I just want it to stop.

Dad has everyone leave, and he sits next to me and begins talking. His voice sounds muffled to me as though he is submerged under water. I think Dad's drowning, and I begin to cry. Dad assures me that he is fine. I reach out my hand to see if his skin is wet.

I notice he is sitting in Mrs. Taggart's chair; she is the principal of my school. I tell him he better get out of that chair before she gets back or he will be suspended. Dad tries to orient me, but this is real and cannot be fixed by reality orientation.

That evening, my parents are watching TV, and I am getting some much-needed sleep. All of a sudden, I sit up and look at them. Excitedly, I tell them, "I saw Jesus." Of course, they are listening intensely as I spoke this. "He was standing in the flames and was looking right at me. He pointed to me and said, 'You're the one!'"

Mom immediately believes Jesus was telling me that I am chosen, and she truly believes he has a plan for me.

The next day, I attend aqua therapy with Laura, and my sister Courtney is with me. I enjoy swimming, and Laura says it helps my muscles and anxiety. I swim for an hour and feel very relaxed. We change and go on our first outing, which is a nearby café. Ricky and my parents are with us.

I feel very uncomfortable. It is a busy place, and I don't want to be here. I point to each one at the table and say, "I hate you and you and you." I then tell them that I want to die and that I am going to kill myself. Needless to say, it didn't go well, and I return to my room and hide under the blankets.

I am awakened by the extremely loud beeping of the IV and try to grab it and push it over. I pick up the phone on the nightstand to call 911 to get me help to get away from this noise. Mom plays music at a very low volume, and it calms me down for a little while.

That evening, my parents are watching *Wheel of Fortune*, and I jump up, believing I am actually a contestant on the show. I guess letters, thinking I will win money if I get the puzzle correct. I ask my parents to help me win so I can win a trip to Italy. One of my favorite places has always been Tuscany. It's beautiful, and I hope that one day I can visit this place.

I try to get some sleep, but then I jump up out of bed and start wiping my skin frantically to get all the insects off my skin; they are all over me. I see spiders and ants crawling everywhere. I yell for them to change my sheets and wipe my bed down.

The next day, I am irritable from not sleeping, but Mom insists I take a shower. As I enter the bathroom and look at the shower chair, I panic and ask Mom why she wants to kill me by putting me in the electric chair. Mom sits me down, and I scream for help so that I am not electrocuted.

After my shower, I take all our makeup and toiletries and throw them across the room. Again, I look at Mom and ask her, "Who are you? You are not my mom." And I begin hitting her as though she is a stranger who is out to harm me.

I am now permitted to go on outings with my parents. The nurse gives Mom my medicine in syringes, and she will give me the meds through my gastric tube. Mom is so excited to be out of that room, and we go to the mall at Robinson. This has always been a favorite place of mine to shop in.

As I am walking through the mall, I begin to sweat and have chest pain. My heart is racing and feels like it is going to beat out of my chest. I become short of breath. There are too many people here, and I am very uncomfortable. The music and all the lights are too much stimulation, and I have to leave right away. Reluctantly, we head back to the institute.

When we pull up, I read the sign and become very upset that I am in an institution, as I called it. I told them that people must think I am crazy and want me locked up. I feel ugly with a moon face and hair that is falling out in clumps from the Rituximab. I was selected best hair in junior high and have always received compliments. Now I am metamorphosing into a hideous creature.

The next several days were difficult for Mom as I would continually become physical with her. I would insist that she was not my mom, and I would look at her and ask her, "Who are you?" and "Why are you here?" Time and time again, she would have to wrap her arms around me and put me on my bed and hold me down until I would become calm.

I think it hurt her more to hear "You are not my mom." In my mind, I believe this to be true, and that is what hurts her so much is because she knows this is real to me. Mom lost me when I was unconscious and now as well because I do not know her.

At this point, I have great physical strength. I know Mom must be exhausted from defending herself time and time again, but she will not leave my side when she doesn't have to. I have been violent with Courtney and Mom and the nurses but not with my other family members. I couldn't imagine hitting one of my grandparents, and I am thankful that God has not allowed this to happen.

The next morning, I am up at 3:00 a.m. I call Ricky's mom, and when she asks, "Who is this?" I say "It's Jake. Jake from the state farm." Any TV shows or commercials I watch seem to be reality for me, and they seem to be making references to me.

Needless to say, I am irritable today. I grab all my homecoming pictures off the bulletin board and rip them to pieces before Mom could intervene. She is devastated as those are irreplaceable memories. I then grab my tiara and bend it, trying to destroy it. I break a piece off, and again, Mom is crushed. She keeps the tiara and tries to put the pieces of my pictures back together.

Mom looks at the broken tiara and says, " If we ever minimize our priorities and make things that are not important, important, then we need to look at this tiara and remember what truly matters and reevaluate. This will symbolize a time in our lives that God has shown you great mercy."

The next day, it's just me and Mom. Again, I become combative and jump around as though I am in a boxing ring. I talk to her in a threatening manner and call her Emma.

She holds me down on the bed, and the nurses come in. Mom tells them, "It's okay. I have it under control." She asks them to leave as their presence only increases my agitation. I truly believe the scripture that says that God will not give us more than we can bear. I do not know anyone other than my mom who, for almost four months, could handle this type of storm.

Evening comes, and I walk over to the window. We are several floors up, and I open the large double window. Mom jumps up and runs to my side. I look at her and say, "I am going to jump. They are telling me to kill myself."

Mom grabs me and pulls me back to the bed. Several minutes later, I step on the window seat and make an attempt again but to no avail. Mom grabs and bear-hugs me. She puts me on the bed and yells for the nurses to get maintenance in there to secure the window. I am extremely strong at this point of my illness, but what is stronger than a mama bear trying to protect her cub?

When I calm down and lie in bed, Mom goes over to the lounge chair and curls up into a fetal position. She begins to weep. I mock her without remorse and say, "Poor baby, are you crying? Aww, poor baby."

She begins to cry out to Jesus, and I hear her ask, "How is this glorifying you?"

It's a lot for her to handle, but she knows there is a reason. She thinks of Psalm 50:15, which says, "Call upon me in the day of trouble and I will rescue you and you will glorify me."

The next day, I am agitated, and Mom plays music on the CD player. It's only temporarily effective, and then I begin to throw things. I remove the CD from the CD player, and Mom watches as I try to sneak into the bathroom with the CD. She knows I am going to try to cut my throat because first of all she is a mom and secondly a psychiatric nurse.

She begins to safety-proof my room and removes the thumbtacks from the bulletin board that once held my homecoming pictures. She then informs the nurse to bring in tape for my pictures and to also make sure I only receive spoons on my tray.

While Mom is doing this, I remove the chord from the CD player and head to the bathroom. There is a struggle between us, but Mom wins. She removes all sharp objects from the room and also my handheld mirrors.

After I am calm and relaxing in bed, I pull out my journal and ask Mom for a pencil to write in my journal. Mom is wary, but she gives it to me. I write a page and then take the pencil and start digging into my wrist. Mom grabs it and downgrades me to crayons.

After days of schizophrenic-like symptoms and suicidal attempts, I begin to improve daily. The doctor states that this is a long process and that it might take two years for the complete healing of my brain. As my psychiatric symptoms decrease and they see that I am doing better, they begin planning my discharge. I am due to leave on April 10, and Mom asks the doctor to move it up to April 2; she cannot stand me being in that room for much longer. My family is so excited that soon they will be taking me home.

This has been quite the ordeal, and my parents have shown great strength and endurance. They have been a light to others without even realizing it. A nurse came up to my parents and asked them how they could be so strong during this time. Of course, and rightly so, they gave God all the glory.

Hannah's Homecoming

I AM FINALLY going home. Mom is packing all our things. I have never seen her move so fast; I think she's afraid they will change their mind and make us stay longer. I continue to have my gastric tube until I take in more calories. We are hoping this is out before prom.

We are so excited that we will all be back together again. I cannot wait to see Courtney and Davey. Mom says she has a special surprise for me when we get home. Everything is packed. While Dad is putting everything in the car, Mom picks up my tiara and places it in a bag. She looks at it and will always remember this season and the grace that God has shown upon our lives. Spring is here.

We arrive home to the Christmas tree that is still up with packages unopened and under the tree. That was how we left it on Christmas Eve 2013. My family and friends are gathered, and there is Christmas music playing and a delicious dinner on the table. Yes, we are having Christmas in April, and this is the best Christmas ever.

Before I became ill, Mom entered me in the America's Homecoming Queen Pageant. During my illness, Mom ran home to gather up some clean clothes. She glanced on Dad's dresser and saw a letter from the pageant director. She opened it and read that I was selected as a state finalist for America's Homecoming Queen.

Mom set up the arrangements, believing by faith that I would be able to participate. We will be heading to Dayton on April 13 for the pageant. In just a few days, we will be leaving. I will not be ready cognitively. How am I going to sit in interviews and answer tough questions?

Mom insists we go. "If anyone deserves to be America's Homecoming Queen, it's you!"

We are all born and raised in Ohio and have not once been to Dayton. The pageant can be anywhere, but why Dayton? We arrive at our hotel and then grab dinner. After dinner, Mom is tired and wants to head back to the hotel. Dad asks me to take a walk with him. Not too long ago, I was paralyzed, and Dad wants nothing more than to take a walk with his little girl.

Dad sees a bell tower in the distance, so we head over to the tower. It's a beautiful, warm spring day with flowers in bloom, and new life is beginning. As we reach the gate of the bell tower, my dad falls to his knees as he reads the words on the gate:

> And in despair I bowed my head there is no peace on earth I said for hate is strong and mocks the song of peace on earth good will to men. Then pealed the bells more loud and deep God is not dead nor does

he sleep. The wrong shall fail and the right prevail
with peace on earth good will to men.

Dad praised the Lord, and God told him, "I was with
you before the storm, I was with you during the storm,
and I am with you after the storm." This is the song Mom
listened to time and time again.

Seeing this quote on the bell tower gate greatly
increased our faith. When others hear of this, I pray that it
will encourage them as well that Jesus proves himself to be
with us before, during, and after the storm. We just have to
believe by faith that he will carry us.

This pageant could have been in any city in Ohio or
we could have gone back to the hotel with Mom and not
have taken that walk to the bell tower. There is a reason for
everything under the sun, and I know that this was God
taking the time to show us how much he truly cares.

I didn't do well in the interviews, and of course, I didn't
get the title. But I had a wonderful time with my parents,
and after the pageant, I wept. Mom thought I was crying
because I didn't win. I sat next to her and asked, "Did I hit
you when I was sick?"

I did not care about the pageant, and for some reason, it
hit me all of a sudden that I hurt Mom.

She just smiled and said, "I'm fine. You didn't hurt me.
No worries. It's behind us now."

April 25, 2014

My senior prom is here. I am dressed in my white long gown embellished with silver gems. I'm at the gazebo getting pictures taken with my date. What a glorious time at the gazebo! Not too long ago, we were having a prayer vigil for Noah and me. It was a dark time. Truly, this is a time of celebration even though I have a moon face and thinning hair.

I'm excited to walk into the gymnasium of our high school. It's been several months since I have been here. The gym is full of family and friends sitting in the bleachers awaiting the grand entrance of the seniors. I walk in with my date, Donnie.

Mr. Hlivko, who is one of my favorite teachers, announces our names and says, "Hannah 'The Fighter' Leasure!" Everyone in the bleachers stand to their feet, and I hear people screaming with joy and excitement that I am here.

I see my parents and grandparents standing and clapping, and I am so grateful that they did not give up on me. It would have been understood if they had the nurses look after me, but if they did and Mom wasn't there, I might have jumped from the window that night. God had his hands in the situation and still does.

This is the most heartwarming welcome from my community. I am so glad to be home, and I am ready to share my story and to help others in Toronto and throughout the nation.

June 6, 2014

GRADUATION DAY IS here, and it is bittersweet as my Chihuahua just passed away today. But I know she is with Jesus. He would not allow us to love our animals and become attached and take them from us to never see them again. He is a God who gives good gifts, and I will see her again one day.

I am dressed in my white cap and gown. I am able to receive my diploma even though I missed most of my senior year because I had obtained all my credits before I became ill. My family is so happy to see me walk across the stage. It's been a difficult road, but we made it through and Jesus paved the way. This day will forever be etched in our hearts.

I receive a letter from America's Homecoming Queen stating that I have been selected to participate in a halftime show at the Liberty Bowl. I will be dancing with other girls across the nation. At the beginning of this year, I was paralyzed; and on December 29, I will be dancing at the Liberty Bowl.

God gives good gifts, and what could be better than being in a halftime show? Oh, did I say it will be held in

Memphis? I will be able to visit the city and also visit St. Jude's Hospital. My dream will soon be a reality.

I arrive in Memphis, and after getting settled in, all of us girls load up on tour buses and head to St. Jude's. I am able to listen to a former patient speak about her trial and the healing that was restored to her. I make a card for the kids who are fighting cancer and hope that this will encourage them and give them hope. This hospital is a blessing to so many who cannot afford to pay.

I hope to volunteer or work here one day. There is no limit to God. Kids with cancer will always have a special place in my heart. I only had a taste of what they go through with the Rituximab I received. Mom bought me a remembrance necklace. I love the quote by Danny Thomas that says "No child should die in the dawn of life."

Tonight, my parents and I are taking a tour through Memphis in Cinderella's carriage. What a beautiful and cool night! I look up to heaven and thank the Lord for all he has done in my life and for using me to glorify him. He is still a miracle worker, and although I don't understand why God didn't heal my friend Noah, I know that he is walking side by side with Jesus. And while I am here, I will do God's work and know that one day I will see Noah again.

When I hear people say that he lost his battle, I say that he didn't lose anything but gained everything. Be encouraged, all who are afflicted! I was in the deepest, darkest time in my life and I will never regain the two months that I was in an unconscious state, but I intend to make a difference and enjoy every moment given to me. God has a purpose for each one of us. Seek out your purpose and fulfill it without fear, knowing he will lead the way.

I had a friend mock and criticize me for writing a book, but that's okay because in the story of Noah, they mocked and laughed at him for building an ark. But he was obedient to what God had called him to do. Well, this is my "ark," and I want to be obedient to my Heavenly Father. So to any of you who feel that people mock and criticize you, understand who it matters to most and hold your head up high. And to those who are battling an illness or going through troubled times, I hope that I have inspired you to pray and to find that desire deep within to want to live and to find strength in the Lord and in your family. Jesus brought us comfort and a peace that passes all understanding, and what he did for me, he wants to accomplish through you. God bless.

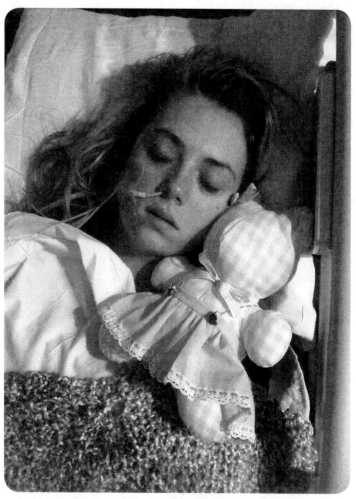

I was unresponsive and had to receive nutrition
through a naso-gastric tube, January 2014

This is a drawing by my friend Noah,
who walked closely with Jesus

The bell tower gate located in Dayton,
Ohio, April 12, 2014

Dad and I in Memphis at the Liberty
Bowl, December 29, 2014

Mom and I at the Liberty Bowl in
Memphis, December 29, 2014

Riding through downtown Memphis,
December 29, 2014

Beverly Hills in June 2015

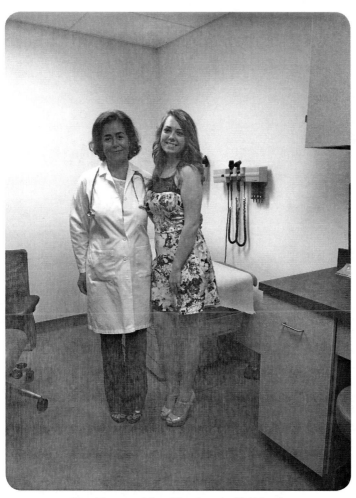

Dr. Alper and I at Pittsburgh Children's
Hospital, August 2015